A NONFICTION

BY

PHAROSE
KING

HOMELESS FORTUNE

MA-17
Not appropriate for minors
Mature Audiences

Mature Readers Only. This book contains graphic storytelling surrounding themes of sexual assault, sex work, violence, and suicide.

ISBN: 979-8-9975613-0-7

This book is a biographical work based on the author's firsthand experiences, insights, and opinions. Certain names, details, identifying characteristics, and events may have been changed or adapted to protect privacy or enhance the narrative. Any resemblance to actual persons, living or deceased, beyond those intentionally portrayed, is coincidental.

This publication is intended for informational, educational, and inspirational purposes only. It is not intended to provide any professional advice. Readers are encouraged to seek guidance from qualified professionals regarding individual circumstances. While the author has made every effort to ensure the accuracy and completeness of the information presented, no guarantees or warranties are made regarding the results that may be obtained from applying the ideas, strategies, or suggestions contained in this book. Individual experiences and outcomes will vary.

By reading this book, the reader acknowledges that the author and publisher shall not be held liable for any loss, risk, injury, or damages, direct or indirect, arising from the use or application of the material contained herein.

Dedication Page

Hi Dad!!

I just wanted you to know that I did it without you. Remember when you took all my stuff to the dump?

That was you telling the universe and the world that you relinquish your lifetime duties as a parent. As most other abandoned children, I literally slept on the streets.

Well, just so you know, a Rose grew from all that. Thank you for all that you have taught me through reverse parenting. I hope reading this helps you find the part of your soul that is missing.

I know you will never get one part back, and that part is me.

Acknowledgements

A big special THANK YOU to my TikTok moms. When y'all met me, you didn't know what you were stepping into. I told you my life gets crazy. I am walking entertainment. I don't know how I do it. I just do it. I never had a close relationship with my family. I was the Black sheep. A victim to household bullying. A witness to domestic spousal abuse. You all helped me to heal the trauma my own family caused me. I love each and every one of you. I am proud of the work we did on that app both on my own channel and the movement/conversations we started. This introspection of healing is for you all. I love you.

-MadamPhysique

Foreword

As a human behavior researcher and therapist, I never saw myself having this much life experience. But what else should I have expected graduating with a bachelor's degree at 19 years old. My parents got divorced and I had no option but to face the world alone. Education was always my best friend. Little did I know that education was making me create a career field and lane of my own. I have gathered outstanding ethnographic research that scientists, psychologists, and sociologists would never ever get.

Because I actually care. I threw myself out there into the wild. I got to know humans in a personable raw way. I put my college research training to good use. I did my best to heal people, even the ones who have hurt me. I am not mad at my rapist. I hate what he did to me. But as an incoming clinical mental health professional and him being a living breathing human I must find a way to put those actions behind me. Nothing written in this book is personal. It is to convey a message of healing to anybody who reads it.

It is time to heal this world, and to do that, every single one of us, including you, must find a way to let things go. We must be the bigger person right now in this moment. That way we can have effective open dialogue. So we can raise the next generation to even greater levels.

My research is not over.

Dialogue

This book is not written to make you think. It is written to make you experience.

Madam is a struggling homeless person. Just recently forced out of full-time work due to having post-traumatic stress disorder while also transitioning from male-to-female she winds up on the streets, from the sandy beaches of Santa Monica, CA to a tent on the sidewalk to be more specific. She faces tears, struggle, and resilience.

Homeless Fortune is not written in chronological order. Each chapter has a specific tone and message relevant to the chapter title to paint an entire picture of the complicated, scattered, and dispersed human mind, memory, and life.

ROSE THORN LOCATIONS

1. Public Defecation
2. Coping with Drugs
3. First Boyfriend
4. Sex Work Fight
5. Sexual Assault
6. Suicide Attempt
7. Existentialism
8. Job Hiring Bias
9. Disabled & Homeless
10. Asian Foster Mom
11. Locker Room Fight
12. Starting New

Table of Contents:

Based on the Viral TikTok Docuseries PTSDocs,

started by @TheMadamPhysique.

"What's the point in holding on to something knowing that it can be taken away? So, you just stop caring. That is the mindset." –Madam

I. Inside the Mind

"Why would anybody want to love me? I'm dirty." -
Madam

Madam has not showered in days, weeks. Her hair is tangled more than a tree's deep roots. She cannot remember the last time she used a toothbrush. When you see her, she probably won't smile back because she does not want you to see the filth in her mouth. So, she stays hidden. She stayed away from the public eye. Because the public is clean. She is dirty. The public is beautiful. She is ugly.

There are many things she believes while homeless but the number one was, "I do not belong." When she got on the bus, she was the biggest anti-Rosa Parks protestor because to the back of the bus is where she belonged. The public didn't deserve to be around her stench. She smelled. She knew she smelled. She has been sweating in this same outfit for days. The public didn't deserve to be around her stench. She is dirty. She's been sleeping in the bushes, so she doesn't get attacked at night. The public didn't deserve to be around her stench. She is ugly. Her aura is dark, dim, she is traveling through the darkness.

The inner City was not a safe place to sleep, especially with the suffering battle of Post-Traumatic Stress Disorder. So, she made her way to the beach. The waves kept her calm. The wind blew strong. Her odor wouldn't be smelled by the public. But one night the sun went down. The public went to their homes. Now it's just her and the beasts of the wild. I mean the beasts of society. I mean the wild beasts that society makes. I mean the dehumanized humans.

There was a city service center on the beach. Madam hid in the shadows until the sanitation engineers finished cleaning and locked the doors. Once they left, she went around back. There was a corner spot away from any lighting. She laid down to rest.

In the distance Madam heard footsteps and voices. Her heart rate rose. Then came sounds of laughter. *"Phew, just some late-night beach goers,"* she thought. If they are out at this part of the beach this late then she must be safe. She closed her eyes and went to sleep. A few minutes later she is struck with a bag. Alarmed, she opened her eyes.

A face emerged over the corner of the building. *"Oh sorry. I didn't know anyone was there,"* a middle-aged

Caucasian male said. *"I'll go find somewhere to sleep tonight."*

In the homeless sub-world, they must do their best to domesticate themselves. One of those things is repetition and familiarity. Think about how important it is for you to get back to your familiar home every night so you can sleep? Madam was sleeping in this person's home and didn't even know. But the fact that somebody already claimed this area was enough to cause her to move. How many others claim this spot and will try to come throughout the night?

The panic ensued. Madam got up and went walking. She checked lifeguard towers, beach bathrooms, behind stores. Nowhere was a good enough location for her safety. After a mile of walking, she finally found her quarters. Walking along the road, she noticed a strip of bushes separating the highway from the beach. She hopped the median and walked over. *"There's got to be an open patch in here somewhere!"* she thought to herself searching for an opening. Then she finally stumbled upon one.

There was a tiny sliver that she slipped through getting cut by stems & branches. The temporary pain led to an empty bird's nest waiting for her to build. Using her hands, she swept up the ground to clear out the loose branches and sticks. The leftover patch was just big enough for her upper torso to lay in while her lower extremities would have to snuggle in the bushes.

"Entrenched rough sleeping signals an almost complete neglect or absence of any core valued self/identity, coupled with a "paranoid" level of distrust" (Seager, 2011). It was this night sleeping on raw dirt in the cold with no sign of a better future that her mind resorted to her prehistoric animalistic instincts. It was this night Madam accepted herself as a reject from society. It was this night that forever degraded her sense of self and humanity. It was this night that the psychological detriments of homelessness began.

Madam laid down staring at the sky for hours. It was cold, yet peaceful. That was…until her peace got disturbed. She had to use the bathroom. Not just urination, she had to take a gigantic poop. She tried to hold it in. That worked for about 4 minutes before her rectum became full and ready to expel. The elders always say, "don't sh*t where you sleep." Following the ancestral advice, she went to find a spot to release her digestion. There was no other opening in the surrounding bushes she could squeeze into. That left one option: the sand on the beach.

She walked out to the sand and made a makeshift outhouse toilet. While defecating, a group of young adults began walking down the beach. One girl had amazing eyesight with a not so quiet voice. She said aloud, *"Is that a homeless person sh*tting?"* Madam became overwhelmed with feelings of embarrassment. This was possibly the most embarrassing moment she has ever experienced in her life.

"There is a massive correlation between entrenched homelessness and severe mental health problems" (Seager, 2011). This incident became the beginning of a downward mental health spiral for Madam. Not only is she defecating in the sand on the beach in the middle of the night, but members of the public were forced to see such a galling act.

"[Homeless individuals] don't come off the streets in truth because of their past experiences and damaged personalities that make them alienated from themselves and unable to relate to wider society" (Seager, 2011). Homelessness completely obliterates the old ways of the developing or post frontal lobe developed mind. It trounces any previous mindset and forces a mode of survival. Once a person is forced to disconnect from the wider society, that mode of alienation and survival institutes.

"My psyche shattered. I no longer knew what shelter felt like. I felt exposed. My sympathetic nervous system was at an all-time high. I would compare my first night sleeping in the bushes as a little kid who saw a scary

movie and could not go to bed. Only, there was no mommy to rock me to sleep. I had to find sleep. I didn't sleep. I didn't sleep for days. Every noise shifted me. Every sound alerted me. I was scared. I felt unworthy."

-Madam

Being homeless starts to deconstruct the mind. You lose all familiarity of previous safety and refuge. You lose touch with reality. You enter a mindset of being subpar, sub-level, less than human. Embarrassment affected Madam the most. How can somebody be *this* rejected from society? From family? From friends?

In Madam's case, she was not rejected. She was simply no longer a part of, which is even worse. Madam was going through a gender identity crisis while at the same time battling first-responder Post Traumatic

Stress Disorder. Her mind was filled with constant flashbacks. She could not walk without seeing vivid imagery and hearing audible hallucinations from the past. To start the healing process, her brain had to be surrounded by new: new surroundings, new family, new friends, new everything. This was not an easy decision but one she was forced to make to get her mental health back to a healthy state away from triggers of the past.

This puts Madam at an even more disadvantage because her mind is already fragile and vulnerable with a present mental disorder and current episode of psychosis. Seager (2011) found that homelessness makes a person alienated from their own identity. Madam was triple alienated from her identity:

1. the identity she once knew was a character that she made to avoid being persecuted growing up,
2. battling a debilitating mental disorder like PTSD, she would be living in the present, but her mind would be re-experiencing the past.
3. now, she was homeless with no end in sight.

Homelessness is an unfathomable human experience. In Madam's situation she was alienated from her identity because your identity can only develop and learn how to exist within a home. The longer an individual is without a home, the further they will drift from the identity they once knew. Little by little the identity of survival consumes the mind. Sleeping outside for the first time ignites a survival identity instantaneously. The most innate human craving is shattered: the feeling of safety.

Who? What? When? Where? Why? How?

Who could hurt me?

What can they do to hurt me?

When could they hurt me?

Where am I that they could hurt me?

Why would they want to hurt me?

How would they be able to hurt me?

These subconscious thoughts race in the back of the homeless mind constantly.

"What's the point in holding on to something knowing that it can be taken away? So, you just stop caring. That is the mindset." -Madam

II. Inside the Body

A lot of people talk about anxiety. A lot of people exacerbate anxiety. A lot of people use anxiety as a scapegoat. A lot of people do nothing to treat their anxiety. The small thought of sleeping outside gives any general person anxiety. That small thought you feel is minuscule compared to the actual feelings of sleeping on the street.

While sleeping on the street your brain forgets what true warmth feels like. Blankets provide a sense of comfort. A feeling of protection. When was the last time you slept without a blanket? Were you cold? Did you curl up in the fetal position? Did you start to shiver? Were you able to get up and grab a blanket?

Being homeless puts a lot of stress on and in your body. Experiencing an avalanche of Post-Traumatic

Stress Disorder symptoms at the same time puts your physical body under even more severe stress. Madam had to find a way to channel all that energy. This early in the PTSD experience, she did not know what was going on with her mind. With every movement she warped into a flashback. With every noise she began to experience visual hallucinations. With every loud noise she experienced audible hallucinations. She would be what they would call "crazy." To the normal world she appeared simply abnormal. She would be mute. She would stay alone. She would be in isolation.

Madam spent most of her time meditating, sitting still in one spot. A favorite spot of hers was Palisades Park in Santa Monica, California. It had restrooms in case she ever needed to go, and there were constant tourists and residents walking around so she could meditate with minimal risk of anything negative happening to her.

It would get annoying when another homeless person would come sit by her, because she wanted to be alone. But she understood their shared pain. We all are trying to process this homeless life differently, and one thing she has learned growing up with that great mind of hers is that some people process better in the company of others and the rest process better in the company of themselves.

Neither route is wrong, simply different roads one takes to get themselves out of the situation they are in. So, she let them. She provided a calming atmosphere that appeared safe, and they would provide her with more physical safety. They were able to sort through their belongings, leave their belongings to go to the bathroom, catch up on sleep they have not had for 2-3 nights. They are both are at the critical point in homelessness where they are ashamed to bring our uncleansed bodies around the general public; it is best if they bond together for the time being.

Just like a human living in normal society, Madam got bored of seeing the same thing over and over again. This meant she had to find more routine spots to spend time at. A little further north of Palisades Park, between Wilshire Blvd and California Ave, there is a large building of restrooms. This place was more of a homeless hangout area. She met a lot of people here. The homeless people spending time here were some of the nicest, most sharing, kind people you would ever meet. After a while, the homeless community got used to her being "the meditating girl." They offered her pillows, marijuana, blankets, food, and sometimes gave her cash. Other homeless people joined her in meditating. A lot of others were catching up on much needed sleep that they have not gotten since they did not know what safety felt like.

Did you notice that during the last couple paragraphs I emphasized the themes of safety and feeling safe to survive? Tell me, what happens to *your* body when you feel unsafe? What happens to your senses? How does your behavior change? What do you do? You go to safety, which is usually home. Now think about the person that does not have a home to go to...

Madam has an undergraduate degree from the field of Sociology: The Study of Human Behavior. Although well-versed in most, if not all, of the main theories, her studies primarily focused on Conflict Theory, Symbolic

Interaction Theory, and Differential Theory. Most narcissists and manipulators try to paint the actions a person does when in an irrational state, "crazy," as their true self. That is nowhere close to their true identity, that is a direct reflection of the conflict they are fighting.

In fact, a Sociologist such as herself would argue that a person's true identity automatically shows when they are in their most comforting safe space. This lowers all the defense mechanisms their brain has evolved to protect them from further conflict. So next time you see a homeless person acting "crazy," Madam would like you to remember that they are acting irrational because they do not feel safe.

"My body did not know rest. I have not slept in days. I rested my eyes, but I did not sleep. My PTSD hyper-

vigilance was in a 24/7 constant state of awareness. Every morning when it was time to get up, my body would be shaking. There were nights I had to get up and walk because the shakes were too severe.

My eyes were constantly scanning. I never got to rest. The only time I could get rest would be during the day when the public was at the beach or walking around the park. Even then, I could not sleep too much because I was still in a new city, and if you are aware of PTSD then you understand that it does not like new. PTSD-brain needs familiarity, so it knows how to predict to stay in control. Only my brain was not in control, everything familiar would bring up a negative flashback. PTSD-brain thinks it knows what it needs but what it wants will only make the condition even worse." -Madam

Dr. David Berceli (2024) is a master in neuro-trauma, conducting teachings across 50 countries. He explains that all mammal species experience trauma tremors. It is a natural bodily stress response. What was unique about Dr. Berceli's research in a bomb shelter is that he observed children openly tremoring, whereas teenagers and adults were trying to control their tremors.

With clinical PTSD, you are no longer in control of your body. Your PTSD is in control of your body. Those control mechanisms that you developed growing up get shattered by a monster so huge, so scary that you have no choice but to tremble, such as Madam. Dr. Berceli ties these control mechanisms as defense narratives that have been developed over time in society, but that is not the way it has to be. He goes on to discuss that wild animals experience tremors but do not have PTSD, however, domesticated animals can show symptoms of PTSD.

Dr. Berceli goes on to explain that all humans could access these tremor-releases on their own, however, the difficulty lies within these tremors overwhelming you from your traumatic past. It is at this point that Dr. Berceli believes professional assistance could be needed. "There is an unconscious resistance to letting go of control," Dr. Berceli. PTSD brings about deep subconscious trauma and forces it to the surface. Once PTSD grows within you, it is telling you that it is time to let that trauma go.

Madam's body would shake for no reason. She would meditate but that would not be enough. Homelessness keeps your senses in constant activation.

It forces you to become more in tune with your senses. Once your senses enter overdrive you reach a new level of human experience that I like to refer to as "living through your senses." The street-homelessness experience brings you back to your primal animalistic nature. Like a lioness in the jungle protecting her child, homeless individuals are trying to protect their inner child: the only piece of familiarity they know.

Imagine the situation that thrust you into survival mode. What did you feel? Do you remember how your physiological system reacted? How long did it last? That is the closest resemblance you will get to someone experiencing homelessness. The shakes are uncontrollable. The twitches are unstoppable. The stressed, thus weakened, bodily systems decrease strength causing you to be prone to sickness.

A painless way to cope with this physiological response of homelessness? Drugs. In the past, doctors prescribing ADHD medication ordered supplements that elevated brain activity. This allowed the brain to match the highly active levels caused by ADHD. Drug-addictive use is used to cope with physiological responses.

For example, "meth" is a very common drug of choice for homeless individuals. Most people assume it is used as a reality escape, but have you ever thought maybe it is used as a physiological coping strategy? Being homeless, your stress hormones are astronomically raised. Your cortisol is excreting past max capacity. This causes an abnormal influx of energy that is extremely hard to "sleep off."

Now, the individual is unable to sleep. They are constantly up and "on guard" due to safety concerns. With one session of meth use, your body now has a reason to be elevated. It is a stimulant. It falsely provides your brain with the energy needed to harmonize with the current ongoing stress. It falsely provides your brain with the excuse of staying awake. This misconstrued harmony between the drug's synchronization to a homeless person's physiology relieves the person from the fetter bodily response that homeless individuals go through.

Another misconception that society has is when homeless people return to the sidewalks. With those suffering from PTSD their physiological system is overwhelmed. The ground is very grounding. We are able to release that energy to gravity instead of trying to harness so much. As a fitness professional and wellness coach I am aware of the positive effects grounding yourself does to the body. How many other wellness professionals do you think are out there homeless? The good thing is that they are in-tune with their body.

"What's the point in holding on to something knowing that it can be taken away? So, you just stop caring. That is the mindset." -Madam

III. Finding Your Soul

Homelessness forces you to discover your true self, the core you, the only part of you that you would recognize. People who struggle to navigate their way through homelessness could be linked to them running from their true self. Knowing yourself and cooperating with your true self will always provide you peace, safety, and a way out.

People who have experienced homelessness has gone through the one thing that the general public will never experience. Something has led every homeless person into homelessness. This is usually in the form of a culmination of events in which one minor inconvenience was all it took to force an individual into homelessness.

When trying to get yourself out of homelessness, the life you lived before will never get you out. That was the life that led you directly into homelessness. Homelessness provides you a total reset giving you the advantage to plan out and prevent ever going back into homelessness because you have already experienced it. Anybody who has taken a sociology class has heard of the term "the revolving door." Homelessness can become a revolving door.

Let me explain. You live in a beautiful hotel with a nice revolving door in the lobby. After your reserved stay, you cannot afford another stay, and you refuse to leave. The hotel staff pushes you out through that revolving door. You have two options: you can either keep trying to go back into the hotel through that revolving door knowing you will just be kicked out to the street again or you can walk the street and look at the different options available to you. There are endless paths for you to get to a new living situation, but all those paths require one thing in common: leave the behavior and/or person behind that left you unable to extend your reservation the first time.

The first hotel is the life/identity you were born with. Everything in that hotel was already furnished and provided for you (bed, clothes, food, water, electricity, etc.). Once that first hotel kicked Madam out, she did not get into a habit of going back through that revolving door. She did not even take the bags they threw out with her. She left everything right there on the street and shifted to a growth mindset.

A lack mindset will force you to crave going back to get what you lost. But at times, some things are better staying lost. To find a new way, Madam had to be surrounded by new. Anything old would lead her straight back through that revolving door. It was time to find a new street. A street that did not connect to that hotel.

Have you ever chosen to take a new way home and you have seen things that you never seen before and they have been there this entire time? Being surrounded by the new or unfamiliar forces your brain to discover new. New ways of thinking, new ways of doing, new ways of living, new ways of being: The New You.

Only for Madam, it was not "A New Madam." It was the Madam that she has been trying to unravel her entire life. That constant feeling that there is something deeper inside of her has finally begun to unravel. Before, she just did not know what that feeling was. That feeling was her soul the entire time.

Madam strayed away from her soul in 1st Grade. She went to public school for kindergarten. She had an amazing teacher, Mrs. Sparks. Mrs. Sparks was the best kindergarten teacher. She truly loved her job. She was reason Madam was excited to start 1st Grade. But her caregivers had a different idea. She was forced to attend Christian School.

Not just regular Christian School, it was a Southern Baptist Christian School. She spent her summer trying on private school uniforms. 1st Grade was isolating. She was the only Black person in her class. The rules were completely unnecessary and biased. On top of it, they prayed every 2-3 hours.

First prayer was first thing in the morning. Second prayer was after Bible lecture, which was also the second subject in the morning. This prayer wasn't your typical "Thank you God for giving me a wonderful life." It was a sermon about how imperative it is to ensure your salvation, every day, five days a week, for an entire school year.

Sometimes during Bible lecture there was an added prayer. The third prayer was right before lunch. During miscellaneous subject lectures, there was another prayer: most times this prayer occurred during science. Lastly, there was a dismissal prayer at the end of the school day. Madam probably prayed more in 1st Grade than most adult humans have ever prayed in their entire life. Now, imagine this happening to you from 1st to 6th Grade, every single day for the entirety of each school year.

It was not until 8th Grade that Madam started to feel her soul again. After begging her caregivers for years to let her attend public school, she finally enrolled in 7th Grade. One year free from the chains of the Christian School Society, she (pre-transitioned at the time) realized she was attracted to men. She developed a deep crush on one of her classmates.

One crush turned into another, until she had to figure out what was going on with her. This sexuality went against everything she has prayed against for the last six years. She categorized herself as bisexual until she finished exploring her sexuality. By 11th Grade she realized that she was not bisexual. She was gay. Gay was the closest thing to explain her attraction to men.

That was, until she continued journeying on the path to finding her soul where she discovered she was a Trans Woman. She was attracted to men because she is a straight woman.

Discovering this about soul was tough. She could not believe it. *How am I trans? That makes no sense. Is that even real? Am I crazy? Oh no, I'm one of those people?!*

Children do not know gender. They just know they are born into a body and walk with their soul until some controlling self-absorbed adult knocks them off their path to the point that society, classmates, and others reinforce this astray. That is what happened to Madam. The man who gave her half-DNA led her astray around four years old, so it was easy for society to reinforce this astray.

Walking on this strayed path continued to lead Madam straight back to the same hotel she was continuously kicked out of. She had to try a new path: the path of her soul. The path that everybody has tried to keep her away from. The path that terrified everybody. The path that made everybody upset. The path that made Madam feel her own internal and eternal happiness. The path that made her feel fulfilled and whole.

Coming back to the present, during the first few months of homelessness, Madam lived in complete isolation. There was no "her" to present herself to the world as. She spent all day and night in deep soul-searching thoughts, deep trauma purifying with lots of tears, lots of cries, lots of self-harm, lots of screams, lots of anger, and lots of hatred. She had to get rid of all that goo that everybody has poured on the path to her soul.

Madam had no money. She did not know anybody. She did not care to know anybody because she was still trying to get to know herself. The only connection she had to herself was through meditation. There was a favorite boulder she found, right alongside the beach off Pacific Coast Highway. This boulder had a flat surface just large enough to sit overlooking the sea.

She got into a cross-legged meditative stance and just sat there. Hunger? It did not matter. Sweaty? It did not matter. She just sat in stillness, for hours upon hours. Sometimes she cried, sometimes she sang. Always, she was alone.

It was out on this boulder that she met a man, Zachary. Zachary was also homeless, kind of. He lived out of his RV. Zachary would watch Madam for hours. He was captivated by the beauty so close to him. One day, Zachary wanted a closer look. He walked out to the sand and just paced back and forth while Madam was meditating. She opened her eyes, and the two locked eyes. It was love at first sight.

Zachary smiled at her, and she smiled back. Her heart began to flutter. Her cheeks turned rosy. Her teeth began to shine. Her face illuminated. Zachary got cheery. Happiness consumed him. Once he got the attention he looked for, he returned to his RV, leaving Madam to heal in private. But he was not far. He made sure to crack the window, keeping his eye off Madam. As a man, he felt it was his job to keep her safe.

After some minutes, Zachary came back outside with miscellaneous things. While Madam sat and meditated, Zachary started doing handyman things. He started with cleaning up his junk. His front yard was dirty. He could not get the girl of his dreams with his place looking like this.

Madam got up to go to the bathroom, the port-a-potty. She and Zachary locked eyes as she walked down the makeshift dirt sidewalk that led to the bathroom. They both had a very curious look in their eyes. She went into the port-a-potty and freaked out. *"Is a man seriously interested in me? What if he realizes I'm trans? What am I going to do, move into his RV?"* After using the restroom, she stepped back outside and walked back to her boulder on the beach. Zachary was sure to position himself along her path so he could introduce himself.

"Hi, I never got your name. I'm Zachary," he said, holding out his hand for her to shake.

"Hi, I'm Madam."

"Wow, I love that," Zachary said as his face lit up. He kissed Madam with his eyes. She smiled.

"Well, I have been here for a while, and I know everybody staying out here at the beach. If you ever want to sleep inside or just get out the sun, just come knock on my door and you can sleep in my bed. I will find something to do outside so you can have time to yourself," Zachary told her.

"Thank you," Madam said smiling. *"I'm going to go back to the beach now."*

"Oh sorry, didn't mean to pull you away from what you were doing. I'm right there if you need me."

Madam walked away. Zachary stared at her from behind. This interaction began instant conversation among the beach residents. Zachary became man of the beach, but little was he aware that the other men were just as lonely as him and all wanted to see who would get the new girl. The game of five men fighting for one girl's attention began.

As Madam walked back and forth along the sand, she could see the men all encroaching Zachary at his RV. It was obvious they were talking about her as each of the men took their turn getting a nice, detailed look at Madam walking on the sand.

A few minutes later, it turned into "National Clean Up Your Living Space Day." All of the men began tidying up their living areas, their RVs, their tents, etc. They can get a girl while homeless, but they could not get a girl if they are dirty.

One day Madam was walking up and down the road just exploring the area. As she was walking back to her favorite boulder a man stopped her. He was white, dark brown hair, approximately 5'10", and a full beard. *"Hi, I'm sorry I haven't introduced myself yet, my name is Marc,"* he stuck out his hand for a handshake.

"Hi. I'm Madam," she said, sticking her hand out. Marc gave her a firm handshake. He had strong meaty hands. A blue-collar worker's hands, very strong, very masculine.

"I live down there at the end in that gray RV. Anytime you want to come over just come give me a holler. You're also more than welcome to sleep over if you don't feel safe out here at night."

"Thank you," Madam said with a smile as the handshake ended.

"You're welcome. So, what brings you out here?"

Madam got nervous. *"Should I tell him I'm trans and trying to transition? I'm sure he can tell. Wait, why does he need to know that?"* was the conversation ruminating in her mind.

"I needed a fresh start," she replied.

"I feel that. I came out here not too long ago. Then some stuff happened with work, I lost my job, and I've been figuring it out ever since. But hey I'm comfy now. If you're

ever hungry, I have a kitchen inside I can always cook you something," said Marc.

Madam was starving. She has not eaten real food in days. Her stomach was empty from 2 for $1.00 sunflower seeds at the nearby gas station. She could really use a plate of food. She could use some carbs for energy. She could use some slow digesting food. The offer was tempting. This is the second man that subtly offered her to stay with him. But was she willing to take the risk?

"Oh, thank you. I will let you know," Madam said as she began to walk away to visit her favorite beach boulder.

Walking back to her camp site, she noticed Zachary outside. He had a look of distaste on his face.

Zachary did not like another man hitting on his woman. In his mind, he had Madam first. Madam was his. As she got closer Zachary flashed a big smile with a wave. Madam returned the same.

Madam was more attracted to Zachary than Marc, but Marc seemed more mature than Zachary. The real reason she did not want to hang out with Marc at his RV was because she did not want to ruin her chance with Zachary. She was keeping her options open. After all, she is recently trans and these were the first two men ever interested in her. There were a lot of thoughts running through her mind.

One night Madam was up late and so was Marc. Marc was outside fixing stuff on his RV. Madam was outside meditating under the stars. Marc did not know that Madam was also outside. After a few minutes, a girl showed up to Marc's RV. *"Who is this?"* Madam thought. Marc's face illuminated. He smiled at the sight of her. His cheeks began to blush.

The girl was pretty. She was about 5'9" with blonde medium-length deep wave hair. She was wearing blue jeans and a t-shirt. After Marc and the girl cracked a few laughs, they went inside of his RV. *Could this have been Marc's sister? Was this a Tinder hookup? Was this a potential girlfriend?* Whatever it was, it made Madam look the other way.

A deep state of dejection consumed Madam, but she still had hope for Zachary. After all, she did not pursue Marc out of hope for Zachary. The next morning, she went out to the sand for her morning walk and meditation. The girl who spent the night with

Marc left around the same time. That was definitely a hookup. The air smelled like sex.

Zachary woke up early as well. This day must have been a good sunny morning to go swimming. Zachary came down and went for a swim in front of Madam. He had a stereotypical Hollister/Abercrombie boy body: washboard abs, thin build, young face. They locked eyes. Zachary signaled for Madam to come in the water. "*No,*" she said chuckling. "*Feels great!*" he yelled. Madam chuckled and continued with her morning walk.

Later in the day Madam was walking up from her meditation spot. Zachary was sitting outside admiring the newly found love of his life. He stopped Madam, "*Hey, what were you doing down there? Just meditating?*"

"Yeah," she responds.

"It looks so peaceful I need to try that."

"It's the only thing keeping me together right now."

"I feel that. I just got a puppy. That's all I have. I haven't shown you her, have I?"

"Nope!"

Zachary goes inside his RV and comes back outside with a puppy. It was a small black and white dog, no more than 4 months old. With the puppy cradled in his arms, he walked over to Madam. The two of them standing together with a puppy looked like the perfect family.

Zachary gave the puppy to Madam to hold while he built a makeshift fence. He built the fence around

Madam implying that he wants her to stay with him. *"Are you hungry? Do you want some water?"* he asked.

"I could use some water," she said calmly.

Zachary went inside and left the door open. Madam took this as her opportunity to see how Zachary was living. The inside of his RV was clean. When you first walked in you were in the kitchen. The next room was the living room which had an L-shaped couch, a 32-inch TV, and a small dining table. In the back of the RV was the full-size bed.

Zachary grabbed a bottle of water from the pack on the ground in the living room and walked back outside. *"Sorry it's not cold,"* he said.

"Oh, it's fine. I actually prefer room temperature. Thank you!" Madam said with a smile.

"Awesome," Zachary stared into her eyes. He was in love. They took a few moments and just stared at each other. That was, until their daughter started doing what children do: ruining the perfect moment. *"Princess, no! Get out of that!"* Zachary yelled at the puppy. He walked over and picked up Princess. Madam took a sip of water during this break. She got scared of love and left to go meditate.

Later in the day, this white car comes speeding down the road. It whips a U-turn and parks right in front of Zachary's RV. A Latina woman steps out of the car fuming. You could see the smoke of her anger oozing off her head. She bangs on Zachary's door. He opens the door, and she storms inside.

"Who is this?" Madam asks herself. She just stared at the RV waiting for one of them to come out. After a

few minutes, the lady comes out, gets in her car, and speeds off. An hour or two later this same white car comes flying down the road, makes a U-turn and parked in front of Zachary's RV again. This same woman gets out and opens her back door. She throws out a hamper and starts slamming clothes on hangers into the hamper.

She must have gotten evicted out of wherever she was staying. Now the question is, who is she? Is she a sister? An ex-girlfriend? A friend? The woman brings her clothes inside the RV, and the two of them stay locked inside for the night.

The next morning the car is gone. Zachary and Madam continue their flirting. *"Okay, maybe it was his sister,"* she says to herself.

That was until she came back later in the day. Wherever she was she obviously got kicked out because she spent the next two days moving in clothes, hangers, shoes, and other belongings into Zachary's RV.

The next morning Madam's morning routine resumed: wake up, meditate, walk along the shore, meditate. Zachary came outside with the dog around the same time. He and Madam locked eyes. Zachary's face ignited. Then, the woman came outside. Zachary immediately shut down and shifted his attention away. This was Zachary's ex-girlfriend, and now they are back together. Madam was crushed. You could see the pain of rejection radiate from her face. His facial expressions changed to embarrassment. This was the last interaction Madam allowed the two of them to have.

Palmer (2004) reminds us of an excellent saying: nearly every spiritual philosophy reminds us that we help to create the reality in which we live. As a child, your reality is created by those with power over you. As an adult, your developed childhood reality is shaped by the institutions with power over you. It is how you maneuver within those institutions that allow you to regain control and reshape your developed childhood reality. Most people do not maneuver themselves within power institutions. They allow those institutions to direct them: remaining in the role that they have always known.

Palmer (2004) goes on to state, "True self will come to our rescue, if we let it." When your mind and body is controlled by forces that are not you, you must call on yourself to come save you from yourself. In doing so, you will have to break down all these forces cluttering the path for yourself to get to you.

Zachary was a cluttering force blocking Madam from getting to herself. With the new addition of Zachary's ex-girlfriend reappearing, that presented a huge obstacle in her way. Madam removed herself and returned to what would allow her true self to come closer: peace. Instead of creating this new reality centered around a man, her true self needed a reality centered around her. Thus beginning her next walk down the path to reunification.

"What's the point in holding on to something knowing that it can be taken away? So, you just stop caring. That is the mindset." -Madam

IV. Where to Turn

Where do we go for help? What if the help does not want us? What if the help is not equipped to handle our disability? Everybody wants to help, but not everybody understands that helping means being universal. The phrase "I can't help you" should never be said.

Madam went to a couple places for help. A couple places tried to get her off the street, but those couple places were not understanding that she was in the middle of a psychotic break. The system is not proactive; the system is reactive. Luckily, Madam has a lot of awareness training and education, so she was able to be proactive with her mental health.

A Los Angeles Homeless Services Authority (LAHSA) worker found her sleeping on the streets.

She approached Madam and brought up the idea for a shelter. This shelter promised was to feel like she had her own room to isolate from triggers as needed. She was hesitant to try. *"Just try it out,"* is what the caseworker told her. Madam told her that it would not work since she did not feel she was mentally stable enough to be in a communal space in the early stages of battling PTSD. Madam fawned and tried the shelter anyways.

When they arrived, the staff did not note that she was a trans client actively on hormones. The staff member checking her in was confused. She knew Madam was a girl, but they had her room listed with her birth sex. The staff got mad at whoever pre-filled the intake form. She made them make space for her in the Women's side. After about an hour, Madam went to her cubicle and got cozy.

Let's start off saying that this was not even a shelter. It was a large makeshift tent. There was not even electricity in the bedroom quarters. There was supposed to be, but the USB-outlets attached to the dry-wall did not work. They could not eat in our quarters to prevent bugs from entering since this was a huge tent sitting on an empty lot The bathrooms were outside. The lunch tables were outside. They were fenced in like a prison.

One day she left to go to the gym. While gone, there was some drama that happened with some of her roommates. One of older ladies was upset that she had to share her living spaces with a transwoman. To describe the extra-ness this lady was doing: her cubicle was nowhere near Madam's. Using the U.S. Map for reference, Madam slept in the southwest corner cubicle in San Diego. This other lady's cubicle was in east Ohio. They were nowhere near each other. Both would have to go out of their way to run into each other in the living space. The bathrooms were port-o-potty's continuously monitored by staff, so what the problem was? Misery loves company.

How did Madam find out? She comes back from the gym, and her homegirl tells her that she had to go off on this lady. Madam said, *"For what?"* She responded that the lady living in Ohio was complaining that Madam was living in the same quarters as her, and that Madam needed to be over with the boys.

Ohio was still in the room standing at a cubicle close enough to hear the conversation being nosy. She began to offer her two cents which led she and Madam to get into an argument. Another older lady came and grabbed Madam and told her that a bigoted mind is never worth the fight. She was right.

Staff came into the tent shortly after saying they heard some ruckus. The situation was already dealt with, so the other ladies told staff that nothing happened, and it was over with. Ohio, upset that the rest of the living quarters was on Madam's side, tried to get Madam kicked out of the shelter. She told staff that Madam threatened to hit her and she was scared for her life.

Madam looked that staff member right in the eye and said, "*Now why would I do that knowing that would get me kicked out and ruin my chance at housing. Also might I add that I just got her hair done with all the money I saved from sex work. What I look like wasting my new hair on a fight?"*

The shelter staff busted out laughing. She said, *"Your hair does look good."* She told both Madam and Ohio to stay in their separate parts of the US Map. Madam told her that everything is good in San Diego, but if Ohio has an issue with what she got going on then she needs to report that to the correct authorities instead of trying to start a coup about the sole transgender in the entire shelter threatening her safety when they are all just trying to get their housing and leave.

About a week after this incident, somebody tested positive for COVID-19. This placed the entire shelter on lockdown: a mandatory 14-day lockdown, no exceptions. Madam tried to stay for a few days, but she simply could not. She needed to go exercise. Her nervous system was over-stressing.

Madam tried speaking to the manager who directed her to her caseworker. Madam tried speaking to her caseworker, but she was always busy. Nobody was listening. They were not understanding that she is disabled and her PTSD symptoms were pushing her to a physiological state of unrest, and she needed to go outside.

One morning, Madam woke up in a flashback. She could not take it anymore. She packed up her stuff and walked out the front gate around 4am. It was dark outside. There was no staff. Security told her that if she leaves, she cannot come back. Madam said that was the point. She left and did not look back.

Madam went back to her campsite on the sidewalk. She set up her tent and cried until the sunrise. Once the sun came up, she walked to the gym for a workout and shower. It was time to start all over yet again. What to do? Where to turn?

Madam reached out to her caseworker and let her know that she left the shelter because they were forcing her to risk exposure and stay on lockdown for a man who tested positive in a separate unit and exercise was crucial to healing her disability. The caseworker never called her back. Madam was alone. She would figure it out.

At this point, Madam turned to the social media app TikTok. She put her trust in the public, not for help but for community. As community does, they came rushing in. Some locals recognized her vlog location and came to her rescue. They brought her clothes, supplies, food, and anything else she needed.

Madam cried to them. She called them "her moms." Because she was their little girl, even the ones the same age or younger than her. Their mother's intuition kicked in, and they now had an adopted daughter that needed help in life. They laughed together. They cried together. They were angry together. Most importantly, they healed together.

Her moms tried to get her out of sex work, but she struggled to let go of the life that had provided her comfort and finances for the last few years. But there was also a deeper reason Madam struggled to let go of sex work. It was not the finances that kept her tied to sex work; it was the unscrupulous validation that she believed to be receiving from her clients. Those men did not care for her, and she did not care for them. But they both gave each other something they both desperately needed: affection, physical touch, and attention.

Things were going well with sex work, until one client gave her something she did not ask for: a punch to the face. This client was one of her regulars, Bobby. On a monthly average he would spend $100 to $300 on her private services. Madam thought this encounter would be just like the others. That was until he pulled out a crack pipe. She had a "no hard drugs" policy, but this time she waived policy since a level of trust was developed with one of her most revisiting clients, or at least she thought.

Bobby put the crack pipe on his leg as to prepare it. He took a bag of rocks out of his pocket and placed it on the bed. Next, he pulled out a piece of what looked to be stringed paper.

"What is that?" she asked.

"Foil," he replied.

The foil looked like an aluminum scrub sponge that one would use to scrub food off used pots and pots. Only the color of this sponge was copper.

"What do you do with it?" she inquired.

"You've never done crack before?" He responded as if the average person has not only tried crack but also knows how to prepare the crack pipe for inhalation.

"No, I don't do that," she responded in homage to Whitney Houston's "Crack is Wack" speech.

"You break off a piece of the foil and shove it in first, so you don't suck in a piece of the rock," Bobby explained.

"Oooohh," she replied.

"When I get it all set up, I'll let you try."

"No thanks, I'm good," Madam said.

"You sure? Have you ever done meth?"

"No, I've only done expensive drugs," Madam replied in an astute manner. She has tried meth before, twice. The first time was with her trans sisters. The second time was with her boyfriend at the time. But she was not going to give her client a way in to sharing drugs with her.

"Oh, I was going to say it's kind of like that, just not as strong and it doesn't last as long," Bobby said.

Once Bobby finished preparing the pipe he took a big hit. On the exhale out came a large white cloud. He took a few more hits before saying, *"Okay I'm ready,"* as he put the pipe down.

Bobby leaned in to kiss Madam. The kiss was emotionless. There was no energy exchange between the two. Madam was not even attracted to him. But he paid exceptionally well for a person experiencing homelessness. She began rubbing her hand all over his beer belly. Her hands carried up to his nipple as she aroused his body. His heart rate began to increase. He took off his shirt, and the interaction continued.

"Can you encroach my anus?" Bobby asked. Out of all the times Bobby has requested services from her, this was the first he has ever asked to be penetrated.

"Are you ready for that?" she inquired.

"I think so. It's not going to hurt, is it?" Bobby asked.

"Oh no. I'm not that big," Madam replied.

"Yeah, I think I'm ready, just go easy since it's my first time."

"Did you prepare?"

"What do you mean?"

"Like did you clean out?"

"How do you do that?" Bobby asked in confusion. Obviously, he has never heard of anal douching before.

"You didn't watch any videos or anything?"

"No. I don't know anything about this."

"It's called douching."

"Like an enema?" Bobby asked. So he does have some idea of anal douching.

"Essentially, just not medically induced."

"No, do you think I need to do that?"

"Maybe. Did you poop today?" Madam asked. Of course he needed to douche. You always need to douche before anal sex.

"Yeah, earlier."

"And what was it like? Was it hard, soft?" This question was essential for Madam to ask. If Bobby had a firm hard bowel movement that sank to the bottom of the toilet, then there was a good chance his fiber intake was fine. The chance of having a feces-catastrophe goes down from 99% to 70%.

"It was hard," Bobby replied.

"And what did you eat today?"

"I didn't really eat," Bobby said.

"We should be good, and since it's your first time my expectations aren't high," Madam replied.

Bobby got into a doggy-style position, and Madam penetrated him. He was a very lousy bottom. He was uncomfortable, very uneasy, and struggled to relax his sphincter and be receptive. But Madam needed her coin, so she finished doing what she was being paid to do.

Once Madam ejaculated inside, she slowly pulled out her shaft. On the top of her glans was a minute piece of dung. Bobby turned around and said, *"Oh, sorry." "It's okay. Shit happens,"* pun-intended Madam replied. Bobby took a piece of cloth and cleaned off his dung from her head. He then used the cleansing bacteria found within saliva to cleanse off the glans.

After sex, Bobby took another hit of the crack pipe. Madam sat waiting for the other half of her payment. He reached in his pants pocket and started counting his money. *"Did you take my money?"* he asked sternly.

"No, what are you talking about? I was just with you," Madam said in confusion.

"I had more than this. You took my money," Bobby accused.

"How many times have we met already? You always have money, have I ever taken your money before?" Madam asked.

"No, but I don't know. When I was laying down you reached in my pants and took my money. I saw you."

"Okay that crack is definitely getting to you because I didn't take your money. This is all the money I have." She showed him the $5o he gave her when they first met for the evening.

"You're lying. You went in my pants and took the rest of my money. I had more money than this," Bobby accused.

"How could I have had time to do that when I was engaged with you, hugging you from behind?" Madam responded.

"I don't know. But I know I had more than this and now it's missing." Bobby knows he did not have any more money. But instead of honesty he shifted the

blame to Madam in attempt to avoid not paying her the rest of the money.

Bobby stood still. The air calmed. It was quiet. He lifted his right fist and punched Madam directly in the face.

"Did he really just punch me? Is he fucking crazy?" Madam said to herself.

Madam grabbed the front of his shirt, left hand to his right collarbone, right hand to his left collarbone. In the blink of an eye, she threw him directly into the ground face first.

Loud Smack was the sound of the ground making contact with his skin.

"Are you fucking crazy?" Madam yelled.

Bop! Bop! Bop! was the sound of Madam's left hand striking the left side of his face.

Bobby turned over, throwing Madam off him. He lunged at her and tried to poke her eyes. Madam dipped down escaping his hold. She kicked him right in the chest.

**Boom!* * Bobby flew back.

"Oh I'm bout to fucking kill you," Madam said.

She exited outside and found a cinderblock. Bobby followed her, still engaged in fight mode. Madam bends down to grab the block. On the way up she uses momentum to spin around.

* *Boom!* *

The cinderblock struck Bobby right in the head. Bobby flew back and tried to run away. *"Don't try to run now!"* Madam yelled. Madam caught up with him and pushed Bobby to the ground. Madam grabbed the cinderblock again.

Bam!

Madam struck Bobby in the head again.

Bam! Bam! Bam! Bam!

Madam struck Bobby again and again and again with the cinderblock until his head split open. Blood spewed everywhere, on the cinderblock, on Madam, on the ground, on their clothes. White flesh appeared on the top of his head.

Bam! Madam hit him again.

Now having an entry point to his brain Madam struck him again. Bobby is screaming, *"I'm sorry! I'm sorry!"*

**Bam!* Madam, completely seeing red, struck him again.

"Madam STOP!" A voice screamed.

Madam knew that voice. It was an extremely specific voice. It was loud. It was sharp. It was strong. It was the voice of her God. On the way down to make her next blow to Bobby's head, possibly the fatal blow, Madam threw the block to the side. She let out a loud scream, *"AAAAHHHHHHHHHH!"*

She got up. *"Why did you have to punch me?!"* She yelled. *"Ughhhhh!"*

Bobby, on the ground crying and covering his gashing wound. Madam went inside and grabbed the first piece of fabric she could find to help stop the bleeding.

"*Here!*" she said, handing him a shirt.

Bobby grabbed the shirt and covered his head to stop the bleeding. Madam stood there towering over him trying to calm down. Bobby cried more and more. Madam felt bad, not remorse, just bad. She felt bad that she lost control of herself, and it almost cost somebody their life.

Once he gouged her eyes, her fight or flight response kicked in. Eye gouging can become a lethal act. She flashed back to her training and met lethal force with lethal force. Madam was trained to eliminate the threat. She would not feel safe until the threat, Bobby, was eliminated. Her brain uses a step ladder to escalate or de-escalate. Bobby used his hands for lethal force. She grabbed an object to match.

Madam calms down enough to examine everything that just happened. Now she sees Bobby as an injured person. Despite her anger towards him, Bobby is still a human. A human that is bleeding out. She immediately jumped into paramedic mode. Madam walks closer to Bobby. "*Let me see,*" she says, moving her hands closer to Bobby's head.

Bobby is now experiencing post-traumatic stress. "*Ahh get away!*" He yells.

"I'm trying to help. You're bleeding everywhere. You hit me. We fought, and now it's over. Let me help. You can't see the top of your head," Madam says.

Bobby relaxes and removes the shirt from his head. He has two major wounds: one open gash on his forehead, and another deep wound on the top of his head near the parietal. Madam grabs the shirt and balls it. She cleanses Bobby's head. The wound is very deep to the point you can see raw white flesh. She applies pressure to the wound and tells Bobby to sit up straight. Her hands are stained with blood, but that is not as important compared to a living breathing human who is on the verge of demise.

"Is it bad?" Bobby asks.

"It's pretty bad. You need to go to urgent care so they can pack it or give you stitches," Madam says.

"Ahh man I can't go home like this," Bobby cries. *"Are you sure it's that bad? I can't just go home and put a Band-Aid up there."*

"No, a Band-Aid won't do anything. You need stitches or a packing."

"Ughhh! What did you hit me with?"

"A block."

"A block?! Oh my!" Bobby says.

"You hit me first. I got scared. You can't be upset about how I reacted to your initial action. You're a man. I'm a girl. Do men hit girls?"

"I don't even remember hitting you."

"Well, you did. You're grown. You'll get over it."

"Do you think I need to go to the hospital?" Bobby asks.

"You might not need to do all that. Urgent care should be able to patch this up."

Bobby steps up and immediately feels lightheaded and dizzy. *"Sit down,"* Madam says. Bobby sits back down. About 10 minutes later he gets back up. He complains about feeling unwell but says he needs to get home.

"I'm going to have my wife take me to urgent care."

"YOU HAVE A WIFE?!" Madam yells.

"Yes," Bobby admits.

"WHAT?! What are you going to tell her?"

"I don't know yet. I just need to get home."

"Okay, bye."

"Do I have all my stuff?"

"Yes, and whatever else you left behind is going into the trash."

"What about my money?" Bobby asks.

"You don't have any money. That's how we ended up here. The $50 you gave me is staying with me. If you dropped anything else I'm keeping it as interest," Madam replies.

"Okay. I gotta go."

Bobby got up and walked home. Madam never saw or heard from him again. After this incident, Madam slowly tried to detach herself from private services. It was getting increasingly dangerous. This was not her first fight with a client, but she definitely wanted it to be her last. This was not her first time on the verge of taking one's life, but she definitely wanted it to be her last.

Without exotic services, where does she turn next in a society that rejects her?

"In the National Transgender Discrimination Survey, sex-working participants were more likely to have a disability. Globally, sex-working trans women face violence…Sex work also has benefits for trans women to support psychological well-being such as gender affirmation, affection, and community connectedness, etc." (Fisher, et al., 2023)

There was no one reason why Madam did sex work. There was a myriad of reasons. First, she was disabled. Every day she was experiencing flashbacks, seeing deceased persons, hearing screams, hearing children cries. Her reality was miserable. Second, she was transgender. How does one cope with body image issues? How is it possible that one is a woman yet has the body of a male?

Sex work provided a level of clarity and understanding that she would not have found anywhere else. Her clients were secure in their manhood, in their identity, in their sexuality. One of her regulars was named Darion. Darion saw Madam weekly like clockwork. He saw her growth from the very beginning of her transition. One day she asked him, *"What is it about transwomen that you like?"*

"Well, it's not just transwomen. I like women," Darion said.

"Well, yeah, but I don't have a vagina."

"You don't. You have a girl cock and that's just as fine."

"Girl cock. I hear that word so much. What exactly does it mean? Why do y'all call it that?" Madam asked.

"Look at it. It's feminine." Darion explained. They both look at her penis. *"The hormones change it. It is not masculine like a real cock."*

"I don't get it," Madam said.

"Do you remember what it looked like when you first started hormones? Because I do. It was bigger, had more visible veins, and had a very dominant energy to it. The hormones make it smaller, and it smoothens the appearance

and it makes the skin more supple. It's feminine. See my dick? It doesn't look like this," Darion explained.

"Oh my gosh. You're right," Madam says.

"See? It's a girl cock. I don't mind it."

"Well, what do you prefer? Trans women or cis women?" Madam asks.

"Personally, I don't care. You're all women. People come in different shapes and sizes. I don't think my dick is ugly so why would I call yours ugly? It's not the same as mine. It actually looks better because it's feminine. I follow my heart. My heart led me to your heart. So now I'm here." He said before continuing his monologue, *"Now, I'm not much of a "balls" person. I'll suck your dick. But I won't play with your balls. That's not my thing. But as a man it is my job to make sure you feel pleasure everywhere. When I*

really took the time to research and examine, I found what I like and why I like it. You're just a girl with a dick. That's fine."

Madam was speechless. Never did she fully understand the modulation that hormones do to the external sexual anatomy of transwomen. She mentioned the waiting period she was on before she could qualify for sex reassignment surgery.

Darion responded, *"Awesome. Then I'll have two holes to play with. I've never seen one before and after. I've only seen it after so this is a new experience for me."*

Darion's secureness in his masculinity was astonishing. When Madam spoke about surgery with some, not all, men they would ask why she would want the surgery. Instead of affirming her gender experience they would affirm her penis. That let Madam know which men specifically objectified her transness, and which men actually saw the word women in trans.

Without sex work, Madam would never have met Darion. She never would have had such a secure man sit with her and break down why men love trans women. It is not that they love trans women. It is that they love women. Darion took the time to research, educate, and explore his attraction to all shapes and sizes of women. This conversation was life changing for Madam. She learned that she is simply another human that somebody wants to love.

"What's the point in holding on to something knowing that it can be taken away? So, you just stop caring. That is the mindset." -Madam

V. Who to Trust?

Our brain seeks to protect us.

Becoming homeless, you travel back to your earliest memories, the people who made you feel safe, feel protected. For Madam, the person who made her feel protected disowned her when the going went rough. The other person who did not make her feel protected but made her feel safe was not in a beneficial state of mind. The adult friends who made her feel safe were not local. Madam only had herself.

The one person she could trust: Herself. But even herself was not enough in the midst of a mental breakdown. She was not in control of her mind. Her trauma was in control of her mind. She had to trust her faith. Faith guided her. Madam became a first responder at the immature age of 19. Five years later, she was diagnosed with PTSD. She already held a lot of anger from the trauma she saw. Now this anger has erupted. A critical mental health condition at 24 years old? A critical mental health condition before the brain's frontal lobe has even fully matured? She blamed the system. She blamed the people voting for this system. That diagnosis radicalized Madam.

Madam met a guy. The first time they met was one year before the rape. This guy knew what he wanted from Madam from the very first time he saw her. One morning Madam was leaving the Women's Shelter with her breakfast. While walking, a man in a black hummer-style truck pulled next to her. His name was Rob. Rob was black, low fade to bald hair, around 5'8", with a retired football player build-not muscular but not thin, not big but not small.

Madam found him attractive; she approached the window. Rob brought up how he has been watching Madam for a while. He has seen her on multiple occasions walking to get food from the nearby homeless shelters. This morning, Rob just so coincidentally happened to be driving down the road and saw this as an opportunity to finally talk to the girl he has been interested in.

Seriously, that is what he told Madam. He asked Madam where she was going and offered to give her a ride. She refused. She did not want this random man knowing where she was camping at. He pulled out a roll mixed with $20 and $100 bills and started counting his money in front of Madam.

Opportunity: A Forced Coincidence

Trust: "I've seen you before. I can tell you are going through a lot. Let me help you by giving you a ride."

Control: A Homeless Person in need of Finances

Madam denied the ride. After a few persistent tries, Rob gave her $80 for whatever she needed and left. They coincidentally ran into each other a few more times in the future. After refusing the hang out numerous times before, Madam felt obligated to finally say yes. This yes ruined her psyche for years to come.

Rob invited her to his apartment, but he did not want the neighborhood to see her with him. So, he brought her up through the rear emergency exit. They walked up the stairs. When they got to the second floor, Madam looked over the railing to see a black woman standing in the middle of the road. She was wearing a purple moo-moo and had her hair wrapped. They locked eyes. The air went silent. This woman gave Madam a look that said, "Girl, be careful." This was not her first time seeing a girl go up the stairs with Rob.

They made it to the 4th floor and turned left out the door. They walked a few doors down, and Rob opened the door to his apartment on the right. He held the door open with his left arm for Madam to walk in. "Ladies first," he said. The apartment was a studio with a kitchenette on the right-hand side. The bathroom was directly across from the kitchenette. The living room had a large 60-inch TV. The bed was draped in white, from the white sheets to the white pillowcases to the white comforter.

Rob went to the bathroom and told Madam to get comfortable.

"*Can you grab me some toilet paper, please?"* Rob yelled.

Madam walked over. *"It's under the sink,"* Rob said.

This conversation on the toilet was their first formal introduction to each other. They both shared a similar ethnic background: Jamaican Americans. Rob let her know that he has been in the neighborhood for a while, so he was familiar with the stress that being trans puts a person through. He told Madam that she had a certain light to her and did not want her to get sucked into the street life like the rest of the

Transwomen he watched the light drain from. Rob asked if she was prostituting. She affirmed. He asked if she was prostituting at the blade in Downtown or the other blade in Hollywood. She told him neither. He smiled, *"Good, if you ever need cash, clothes, or a place to sleep just come here."*

A phone rang, cutting the conversation short. Rob got up and grabbed a shoebox from a cabinet and. Madam was friends with an older lady that also kept a shoebox in a cabinet. She knew exactly what that shoebox meant: Rob was a drug dealer. She asked him straight up, *"Are you a dealer?"*

"Yeah, that's what that call was about. I have to go give this lady something," Rob said. An honest gentleman this writer could describe Rob as.

"So, you're leaving?" she asked.

"Just really quick, we were supposed to meet earlier but things got busy then she ran into you. It'll be really quick, imma just go meet her downstairs, then she'll be right back," Rob explained.

"Get comfortable. I'll be right back," he said. This is the second time he told Madam to get comfortable. Why was he so obsessed with Madam needing to get comfortable? He grabbed the TV remote and put on something for her to watch while he stepped out.

A few minutes later, Rob came back. He emptied his pockets and took off his shorts. While counting money, he tells Madam to come over. Their conversation resumes. He's asking her questions. She's asking him questions. Their connection begins to illuminate. Could Madam have finally found a boyfriend? They begin to kiss. To note, Rob was not the best kisser. There was no emotion behind the kiss. He reaches down to her genitals. Madam grabs his hand stopping him.

"It's okay. I like that," Rob tells her referencing her having a penis.

"I don't want to do all that," Madam tells him.

"Just relax," Rob commands.

"No," Madam says while shifting her posture away.

Rob grabs her arm and holds her against the counter and says, *"I know a lot of people out here. A lot of people that can do stuff to you. Just relax, I don't want to have to do that."*

This grown 40-year-old man just threatened a helpless homeless trans woman to coerce her into sex. There are various reasons why men rape. This rape was a case of power. The questions he asked Madam at the very beginning of their date was not to get to know her. It was to determine the power dynamics he was working with. Madam so happy that a man was even interested in her as a Transwoman was oblivious. She could not see that this man was comparing their lives simply to judge how he could overpower her.

When in fear there are three primary responses: fight, flight, or freeze. This man took her fight away with a threat. This man took her flight away by grabbing her arm. Only one fear response remained: freeze. Madam escaped her body and distanced herself from the trauma about to occur.

He reached down her pants and grabbed her penis. His hands were cold and rigid. They feel like they have not been moisturized in days. He pulled down her pants and got on his knees. He put the tip of her penis to his lips and opened his mouth. He began giving fellatio to Madam. Her penis failed to erect. Trying to get her penis erect, he sucked harder. The suction of his mouth became more tense.

Madam picked a spot on the wall and just stared until it was over. He got up off his knees and grabbed her arm guiding her to the couch. He pushed her down to sit and got back down on his knees. He began giving fellatio again. She was still unable to erect. Disgusted and horrified, she realized the television was still on. She could at least watch the *Martin* re-runs as a distraction.

After what felt like hours, Rob got up. He told Madam to take off her shirt as he simultaneously pulled off her pants and panties. Next, he took off his clothes. Rob grabbed her legs and put them in the air. Rob's erect penis slow tried making its way to her anus. The length of his penis was approximately between 7.5 inches. His penis was circumcised. The girth was approximately between 3 inches and 4 inches. He tried to put the tip in. Madam's body was rejecting it. *"It's not going to fit,"* she said.

"Yes, it will. Just relax," he told her.

"No, it's too big. I'm telling you it's not going to fit," she responded.

"It will. Just relax," he said.

He used saliva as his lube, and no, he did not use a condom. He tried a thrust insert over and over with failure each time. *"I told you it wasn't going to fit. I know my hole,"* Madam said.

"It's the position. C'mon let's move to the bed," he said. It was not the position. Anal sex is something your body has to be fully relaxed to receive.

Rob grabbed her arm and pulled her over to the bed and told her to lay on her back. He organized pillows to help prop up Madam's body at an angle. He tried again for penetration. Using saliva, he tried to thrust again. Madam's body rejected him. He used more saliva and thrusted again. This time he was able to make it past the first sphincter muscle, the voluntary one.

His thrusts had worn out the muscle to the point it conceded to his attacks. He tried to go in farther. He used more saliva and thrusted. A sharp pain surrounded Madam' anus. After a few more thrusts he reached the inner involuntary sphincter muscle. Her body rejected his penis again, and he could feel it. "*Relax*," he said.

"*I can't. It's not going to fit. I'm trying to tell you*," she said.

"*I'm already in. I just need you to relax*," he responded.

"*No, you're not in. I can't open that big. I don't take big penises*," she said.

"*My penis isn't that big. It will fit. Trust me*," he said.

Trust you? Trust you? Did she just hear those words come out of his mouth? Just five minutes ago that same mouth threatened her into having sex with him? Trust you? The person who doesn't even know how to properly relax the anal sphincter muscles for penetration? Rape is not okay. But the least you can have some decency. Where is the decorum? Where is the integrity? Where is the honor? Where are the values?

You can at least try to make the experience a little more comfortable for your victim. You are practically raw-dogging a 4-inch girth penis into a tight anus that was not properly prepared to become receptive. If you have ever had anal sex before then you know saliva is not a proper lubricant. You sir are a black man. Was there no lotion?

After a few thrusts Rob stopped and said, "*This is not going to work,*"

"*I told you,*" Madam said.

"*Here come here,*" he grabbed Madam and brought her over to the couch. He climbed on the couch with his knees on the cushion as his upper body rested on the frame. "*You do me,*" he said.

Rob grabbed a condom from the table. "*Here put this on,*" he said handing Madam the condom.

So she must put on a condom to protect you, but she does not get the same grace and consideration from you? How twisted can your mind be? With his glutes aimed sky high, Madam played back the day in her mind. Something highlighted: when Rob used the bathroom as soon as they entered the apartment, he did not have to poop. He was douching his colon. Rob already planned for the two of them to have sex.

Madam put the condom on and tried to penetrate Rob. *"I can't get hard,"* she said.

"Let me help." He turned around and began sucking and touching Madam penis and scrotum. He gave her a hand job and massaged the scrotum simultaneously.

As soon as Madam got an erection, he immediately turned around still holding a firm grip on her penis and guided her penis into his anus. It felt like her penis was caught inside a Chinese Finger Trap. As Madam was thrusting, Rob was masturbating. After a few minutes he ejaculated. He pushed Madam off of him.

"Did you cum?" He asked.

"No, it's okay, I'm fine," she said.

"You sure you don't want to cum?" Rob asked.

"Yes, I'm fine."

"That was fun. We have to do that again."

That was fun? What was fun? Putting Madam through uncomfortable failed anal sex attempt or threatening a harmless girl until she assimilated to having sex with you?

"Here," he said giving Madam her clothes.

She slowly put her clothes on, still in shock that she was just raped. *"Hurry up. I have to run,"* he said.

Madam put on her clothes and began walking towards the door. He stopped her before she could walk by him. *"Hang on, I got some money for you. Help you out a little bit."* He gave her $80.00. Eighty dollars. *"Whenever you need some money, just come to me. I'll have some for you. You know where I live, and here take my number."* He gave Madam his number. Madam listed his number under "rapist." She took the money and left.

For the next few days, Madam sat in silence and isolation. She stayed at her tent in utter pain. There was no way around these feelings. She had just gotten raped. All of her autonomy, her sense of choice, was gone in the midst of a second. How could a human be so cruel? Do you need sex that bad?

After a few days of isolation, Madam remembered her TikTok family was looking for her. She told them goodnight every day so for her not to post was unusual, they thought the worst. She began receiving messages of concern. She turned her camera on and told them what happened.

Most would wonder why Madam did not call the police. What exactly would that do other than put her safety at risk? Research data surrounding sex workers is minimal most likely due to the private nature of sex work and the low reportability of sexual assault.

Sanders (2001) researched data and found a commendable study of active women sex workers. Ninety percent (90%) of the workers in this study reported sexual assault by male clients with thirty-two percent (32%) of that ninety percent reporting a legion of sexual violence encounters by different clients.

Sanders (2001) found that the percentile of violence disclosed from this study were compatible with percentiles found from outreach projects. From the study it was found that the chance of violence was an everyday risk that sex workers assumed.

Could this assumption be due to misogyny? Could the pronounced self-acceptance of such a barbaric act be linked to childhood trauma intensifying complacency?

"What's the point in holding on to something knowing that it can be taken away? So, you just stop caring. That is the mindset." -Madam

VI. Why to Live?

Madam gave up. She had enough. She was sick of being hungry. She was sick of being belittled. She was sick of being judged. She was sick of feeling unsafe. She was sick of being denied. She was sick of being dehumanized. She was sick of humanity. She was sick of trauma. She was sick.

Way back in 1954, Henry and Short launched the Economic Theory of Suicide. This is discussed through the lens of a frustration-aggression model. In the study of human behavior, Conflict Theory has become a prominent theory to not justify but provide reasoning for why certain behaviors happen and/or persist.

At an elementary school comprehension level, Conflict Theory asserts that individuals behave and act in a way out of frustration with a micro and/or macro system. Henry and Short's Economic Theory of Suicide mimics this Sociological Research.

They explain that suicide occurs out of frustration of an individual's attempt to achieve their own social goals thus harvesting aggression in which they act out in either themselves leading to suicide or others leading to homicide.

As a fellow Sociologist, Madam would add more context to their research. Instead of revolving action around a social goal, she would deposit suicidal actions to revolve around a physiological-economic standard of living. Social goals entail the need to bond with society, and many individuals like herself grew up isolated from society.

Madam had no social goals; she had a physiological-economic standard for her way of living. She struggled to maintain and attain that way of living, which led to inflamed frustration within herself, with those responsible for her trauma, with society who is supposed to be there for each other.

Her physical standard of living would be to be healthy. Her health was subliminal. She hadn't been eating. If she was eating it was those packs of sunflower seeds that you can buy at the gas station 2 for $1. Sunflower seeds provided her with ample protein in small amounts. She would get carbs from the trash. Because she was out on the beach, there were a lot of events on the weekends. On Independence Day, there were fireworks off Santa Monica, and the beach pizza businesses were booming. The trash cans would be filled to the rim. There was this one trash can filled to the rim with a perfectly good half-eaten pizza resting on a clean paper plate. The person who placed this here must have OCD like a lot of us because it was perfectly placed in the center of the overflowing trash can. She needed carbs. She needed energy.

Is she really about to eat out of the trash? Is she that low in her life as a homeless person? Well, it would just be like your friend not finishing their slice of pizza, so you eat it. You do not share DNA with your friend. She and thus person could become friends in the future and she'd eat after them.

This is the justification she had to give herself in order to feed her body the energy it needed. "*After all, it is not technically in the trash, it is resting on top, nothing else is touching it,*" she said to herself.

Madam picked up the slice of pizza and kept walking as if it were hers. Well, it was. She peeled off the edge with the bite marks and ate the crust. The carbs revitalized her. Eating leftover food out of the trashcan does something to your psyche. Madam's psyche was already at an all-time low.

Her psychological standard of living was to exist without having any more flashbacks. PTSD was eating her alive, literally. Every day she could feel it peeling her brain. Piece by piece she lost a working fragment to this disease. She had been struggling with undiagnosed PTSD for years and was unaware. Madam went and saw her first therapist in 2018, just about a year on the force. She didn't know what to expect out of therapy, but she knew she needed to be there.

Madam was having the weirdest dreams. She would randomly have these memories playing of deceased people. Her mind would just replay them. This is nothing a 20-year-old should be going through. This therapist simply compared Madam's experience to others that she has helped through therapy.

The therapist told Madam a lot about fire fighters that have sat on the therapy couch and broke down in tears about the imagery they kept seeing. What did those fire fighters have to do with her trauma? Absolutely nothing, but it was enough for her to insinuate that Madam needed to "man-up." She told Madam to go outside and look at all the beauty in the world. *"Go look at flowers. Go touch the grass. Whatever happens at work, leave it at work. Work is gruesome, but the world is not,"* is what the therapist said.

Madam took her advice. She ignored her trauma. She ignored her trauma so hard that within the next year she became a full cocaine addict. By the end of the year, every time she would sneeze, she'd taste cocaine. Cocaine was her drug of choice. In moderate amounts, she could manage the comedown. Her addiction got worse. For work, Madam had to wake up at 4:30AM to put on her uniform and make it in time for the start of her 12-hour shift at 6:00AM. How did she do it? Cocaine. She was an addict.

Madam partied hard. She did whatever she could to distance herself from the trauma in her brain. She went out Wednesday night, Thursday night, Friday night, Saturday night, and Sunday night. That is five nights of cocaine and alcohol use. There were nights she went out and had to wake up in 2 hours for a work shift. How did she stay up at work? Cocaine. She was an addict.

When COVID-19 came, the entire world shut down. With no ability to go out, that craving for cocaine still lingered. Madam realized the weight addiction had on her life. She would be the only one illegally driving on the road to her dealer to pick up a new bag. By this time, she had already quit and started a new job as an Insurance Adjuster for Liberty Mutual. Her addiction just followed her into this job. When the world shut down, she worked from home. It got awkward snorting lines of cocaine to just be high in her apartment. COVID-19 made her do a lot of self-reflection. Madam decided to become cocaine sober. But the addiction was still there, she supplemented her cocaine usage with more alcohol. It got awkward getting drunk alone in her apartment every day, so she stopped drinking too.

About two months after she sobered up, all of her trauma that she vented about in therapy in 2018 came right to the surface, but 20x stronger. She lost control. She did not know who she was. How could she have "the thing" veterans have?

Her psychological health got so bad that she went on short-term disability from work. She could not return back to work. She was fully disabled. She had to adjust her psychological standard of living to be one of living with a permanent mental disability.

The frustration of living with a permanent mental disability was too powerful. The aggression that arose was incalculable. In 1965, the reported suicide age for people between 15-24 in the United States was 9.9% (Haherrhersh and Soss, 1974). Madam blamed everybody, her dad, her old bosses, her old bullies. She blamed herself for being alive and having to go through that childhood development. What was worst was her brain determined PTSD to be the infection needing eradication. The only way her brain could survive would be to shut down.

What could help prevent her brain from shutting down? Better finances since her disability was running out and her job was trying to force her to come back. Thus, leading us into our third analysis of the Physiological Economic Theory of Suicide: Economic Class.

Madam did not need just simple trauma therapy. She needed a specialist, not just any specialist, a specialist specifically trained to process trauma as deep as the trauma she was experiencing. A specialist who has had to do Trauma First Aid. A specialist that has had to do CPR. A specialist that understands the psychological militaristic programming that this system placed in her brain. A specialist to help her turn that switch off. Where are these specialists?

They are secluded. They are attached to the system, or they are running private practices. Because she was no longer part of the system, she could not get help from the system. Her only other option was privatized help. But because she was homeless, she could not afford these specialists.

If Madam does not even have the economic means to afford a $3.50 cheese pizza on the beach, where is she going to get the economic means to afford a $200-

$400 session with a privatized combat-specialist mental health professional? The frustration is just leading to more and more aggression. The flashbacks are getting worse. The cortisol levels are continuing to rise. The hyper vigilance is only getting worse. She is a walking ball of aggression that needed to be released.

Henry and Short were correct in her aggressive feelings being directed towards others resulting in homicide. The blame that she held towards this system and those within it was so strong. it reached its peak. She would study officers. Because she was homeless, they would not pay any attention to her. Which one can she fight and overpower??

Madam would map out every scenario possible. She'd revert back to training, defensive tactics, and crisis control. She even considered committing suicide,

suicide by cop. One night she called 911 for help with a mental episode. she told them she was going to commit suicide. The dispatcher was a woman. She was of no help, or maybe that was the training they received to handle suicidal callers.

The dispatcher tried to give Madam a list of resources she could use. Madam told the dispatcher she was homeless and would at the least need a ride to a psychiatric hospital. The dispatcher told her that they do not offer those types of rides.

That's interesting considering California passed the Lanterman-Petris-Short Act in 1967 which authorizes police officers to commit somebody to an involuntary 72-hour psychiatric hold. However, maybe this dispatcher's willful ignorance was the Universe's

Protection of Life, either Madam's or the officer who would have responded...

The next day, Madam attempted suicide.

"What's the point in holding on to something knowing that it can be taken away? So, you just stop caring. That is the mindset." -Madam

VII. Faith

Everything is going well. You are traveling on the interstate. There is mild to no traffic. "The sun is shining. The birds is chirping" *(Viral TikTok Sound)*. Suddenly, you reach a traffic jam. There is a construction worker redirecting traffic to make sure everybody gets to their destination safely. They are wearing a bright highlighter color vest. They are not trying to prevent you from getting to your destination. They are not toll workers. They are letting you know how to safely navigate through the traffic jam of life.

No human should ever be a toll worker in your life. If a human is asking you for tolls, then you are under control, possibly abuse.

Religion was never suitable for somebody like Madam. She was transgender. The religion she was raised in condemned people like her. When life turns at its worst, people lean into religion. But for Madam, she did not have a religion to lean into. She turned to faith and spirituality. Being transgender is not an easy decision made overnight. It is a process with lots of tears and lots of struggles. She had to find her inner core. She found that through faith.

Washington, Moxley, Garriott, and Weinberger (2009) explain that expressions of faith illuminate a road in which African American women could examine the past, look at the present, and highlight opportunities in their future. They also found that prayer was able to illuminate traumas and forge an emotional healing process for them to recover. More interestingly, the study goes on to explain that human agency must believe in one's own power to bring about a desired outcome: such as leaving homelessness and never returning to homelessness. In interviewing these African American women, the researchers found that the physicality that led them to homelessness would have also ravaged even the person with the most control.

A specific case discussed in this research is an African American woman named Ms. Peters. Ms. Peters was a lot like Madam. Ms. Peters is probably a lot like you. She did not consider herself a spiritual person. Her life was not faith centered. However, she knew that faith was an essential salient resource in her life. This is where Madam was at in her life: faith became an essential resource to her life.

Madam was spiritual, but there was no belief system she felt would accept her. She felt repelled by Christianity. She felt expatriated from Muslim religions. She felt ostracized by the Motherland of Africa. So where does she go? Where would she be accepted? Humans cannot function in isolation. We are natural social beings.

That sense of belonging had to be found within herself. The soul searching began. Who am I? What is life? What is faith? How does one confirm themselves? How does one know they are on the right track?

These existential questions have wandered through the minds of every human. The sooner humans explore their own existentialism, the more love and happiness can be brought into this world. When humans reject or do not consider their own existentialism, it is easier for them to reject or not consider everything about another person's existence, thus leading to hate.

We start with the first question, "Who am I?" Well, who are you? and you? and you too? Who are they? This question is subconsciously asked at an early age. If you grew up with siblings it is much easier to find the answer since you have different personalities to absorb, reflect, or discard. If you are an only child or the eldest, then the need for having external social connections are crucial to finding the answer to these questions. We understand who we are by acknowledging what makes us different yet the same in relation to others.

Mostly every adult goes through their rebirth cycle, if they allow it to take place. This is the stage when your ego is finally mature enough to believe it has successfully raised the person it was assigned to protect since birth. For a lot of people, this usually occurs during the growth of healing from traumatic events or traumatic core memories. For others, this could occur when you finally reach a destination you have been working towards for decades so now your ego feels satisfied and retires.

During this rebirth cycle, those same early childhood questions you had has more formal vocabulary to answer those questions from within the self. "Who am I?" This process begins starting with analyzing family traits, then friends, then the reflection of the self. Most people make drastic changes to their social circle because they realize that social circle was simply a protective factor for their ego. So, who are you?

Madam did not know who she was. She knew she was a person. She had a body. But she did not consider herself a human yet. To be a human one needs an identity. The search for identity began. When you do not have the answers you can find them through a higher power, a teacher. She started with prayer, one of the first things she was taught as a child. I guess there was one thing she could thank from being a Christian School student.

Through prayer, the answer to her identity was revealed: there was no answer because you are forever evolving. This not knowing who she was, was a critical step in the rebirth process. She was not supposed to have formal vocabulary explaining it.

There was only one way to go: Forward. Nobody said starting over was simple. It is also not easy for a third-party to grasp the depth of starting over. The last time the average person has truly started over from scratch is typically never. She had nothing and no one. Every fabric of clothing, every item, every dollar, all came from a new source. The last time the average person experienced this was childbirth. By the time the child brain develops for memory storage the child already has clothes, toys, snacks, family, and usually friends (daycare, school, cousins, etc.) Fully starting a new life as an adult is much different.

The closest representation that I can think of to relate to this level of starting over would be a person who has successfully escaped a domestic violence relationship. They typically escape with nothing but the clothes on their back. They end up on the doorsteps of a shelter with a small bag and an unknown future. They spend the night on a thin mattress surrounded by fear. Fear of being found. Fear of being harmed. Fear of making the wrong decision. Fear of being safe.

Domestic violence survivors relocate to a new city or on the other side of town. They typically do not know anybody. They cut off all ties to avoid their abuser finding them. They had to find a new route to obtain and maintain finances. They had to get new clothes. They leave their abusive relationship with nothing but faith. Faith that things would work themselves out. Faith that they were making the right decision. Faith that life should not be miserable. Faith that one day they will be happy.

Starting over is for the weak because the circumstances they were in drained every ounce of strength from them. Their strength was being poured into a system, a person, or an entity that was happily sucking them dry without any form of reciprocation. All that is left is weakness, defeat, tears, and emptiness. But forging through this starting over process they discover their strength, and that strength is of a magnitude they could not see they possessed.

You see, before they did not know their strength. They only knew their resilience and knowledge. Now they are gaining the skills to turn that resilience and knowledge into strength. The strength to say no. The strength to walk away. The strength to speak up for themselves. The strength to live a life filled with truth and freedom. So yes, starting over is for the weak, because they have been beaten down and drained until there is nothing left for them to give. But during the healing process, they discover a strength that no human could ever match. That strength is developed through faith that they will make it through, and that is a strength that even the toughest of humans fear.

"What's the point in holding on to something knowing that it can be taken away? So, you just stop caring. That is the mindset." -Madam

VIII. Work

Being able to obtain work was very hard. Clinical PTSD leaves Madam at a disadvantage in the workforce. There are certain jobs that she would not perform well in due to this disability. The best field would be the field that helps nurture her disability. The gym is a familiar place that is considered a safe space for her PTSD.

One time she had this amazing interview to become a personal trainer at Planet Fitness. The manager loved her. The interview went so smoothly that the manager wanted to hire her on the spot, but she still had interviews lined up with other candidates. At the end of the interview, the general manager asked where she lives to assess her ability to get to work on time due to the strict schedule.

This question led into Madam revealing her status as unhoused. The manager's facial expression changed from excitement to worry. She reassured the manager that she would be able to make it on time every day. The manager decided not to hire her. If only she knew that Madam had the support of hundreds of thousands of followers ready to support her getting suitable work so she could get off the streets.

What did Lady Gaga say? They can close 99 doors in your face, but all you need is that 1 to open and let you in. Madam got another job interview at Ultimate Performance. The phone interview went super well. She was offered an in-person practical assessment. When she arrived at the training studio, she learned that this was a group practical instead of an individual practical. At the beginning of the interview everybody introduced themselves and the manager led them to the locker room to place their belongings.

Madam went into the women's locker room with the rest of the women. She came out of the women's locker room with everybody else to the managers standing there waiting. Now it was time to be paired with a partner. To avoid any sexual assault claims, the partners were assigned via gender. Madam was partnered with a woman.

Each group started at a different station, and each station was assigned a different manager for scoring. The first station Madam and her was at was being scored by a male manager. There was a language difference about the exercise this manager wanted them to perform. Both Madam and her partner were confused about what the exercise labeled "Hip Hinge" was in front of the back extension machine. Since they were both confused about the exercise the manager had no choice but to explain it.

When describing what to do the male manager looked at Madam, did a full body scan from head to toe, then looked her directly in the eyes and said, "so **he** is going to..."

Her partner and the surrounding groups immediately gasped and looked at her with empathy and compassion. Madam wore skintight leggings and a tight fitted active top. Her breasts were showing prominently through the top. With the groups split via gender the manager had no reason to deliberately misgender Madam. She was shaken up. Her brain flooded with thoughts. *"Am I safe here? Is the company welcoming of trans individuals? If I correct him will bias impact my score? What do I do?"* Madam responded out loud with, *"I'm trans."* The male manager responded, *"Oh I'm sorry I couldn't tell."* Really? You couldn't tell? So, men just walk around in leggings with no bulge showing & big breasts sticking out of their shirt? This author calls horse manure.

This interaction threw Madam off for the rest of the practical examination. She could not focus. How could he not tell? You saw her when she first walked in. You showed everybody to the locker rooms and watched Madam go into the women's side. You saw her exit the women's locker room, and the groups were split via gender to avoid sexual assault risks. How could he not tell? Horse manure.

Madam did the best she could during the practical assessment, but it was not good enough. The next week

HR informed her that she was not selected for the position. She responded to HR and let them know about her experience and how that skewed her performance. HR was very apologetic about her experience and informed that the male manager was not in line with their policies and offered her a secondary retake interview. For this second interview it was going to be with a woman manager and that male manager would not be involved in the process at all.

When the woman manager reached out to her, the email did not seem sincere. Instead of giving her another chance to demonstrate her coaching abilities, this secondary interview was made to be nearly impossible for an entry level trainer. She had to give a presentation on nutrition and be able to answer specific questions about navigating different clientele.

This special interview was 10x harder than the practical interview where they just took each other through workouts.

It was obvious that the managers at this location were mad that Madam reported her behavior. If they did hire her out of fear from HR, the team would just ostracize her until she quit. Either way, the environment was already toxic towards Madam. This retake interview made it obvious that the managers were retaliating against her for making a complaint to HR about sex/gender discrimination.

All Madam needs is one door to open. She had another job interview at a different Planet Fitness location to become the personal trainer. The interview was amazing. Again, the manager really loved her. They dwindled the candidates down to her and one other person, a white male candidate. Who ended up getting the job? The white male, of course he did. The fitness trainer is the face of the gym, of the company. What would it say to have a Black trans woman as the face of your brand? Of course the white man is a more suitable candidate when you are not aware of your own implicit bias.

Madam was more qualified than the white man. She had more transferable life experience. She had her trainer certificate for longer. She worked in gyms prior. This white man just finished his program, and this was his first trainer job. Remove race and gender from the job application, and Madam was the obvious candidate for the job based on resume alone.

After being rejected yet again for a job as a fitness trainer, Madam could not take being destitute any longer. She needed money. She needed it immediately. She should have landed a fitness job by now. At every chance given she was rejected due to being a minority: racial minority, economic minority, gender minority. This is the reality minorities across the world still face. We can be 10-times better, 10-times smarter, 10-times faster, and yet because that minority status is viewed as "less than," implicit bias brain says we are not a part of the majority and therefore not a suitable choice.

Since none of her interviews worked out, Madam stayed in the sex work industry. It provided what she needed at the: immediate money. She was willing to work while homeless, but nobody would give her the opportunity. This pushed feelings of shame into her psyche, feelings of "I'm not good enough," feelings of isolation, feelings of unworthiness. Sex work gave her an opportunity. The men made her feel good enough. She was not isolated. Her body was worthy to somebody. It gave her a bucket to hold her tears.

Sex work was not only work, it was survival. It provided money to ride public transit. It provided money to buy food. It provided money to buy toiletries. It provided money to pay for a gym membership. It provided money to replace things that broke. It provided money to fund her creative art projects. It provided money to heal.

Just when she almost committed to sex work full-time, another opportunity presented itself: a TikTok content creator. Her follower base quickly grew. Madam had one rule with showing her life as a homeless individual: no panhandling, only charity. She received lots of charitable donations from her followers, and she rewarded them with creative art. Her rise to influencing reached a standstill when the Dylan Mulvaney Bud Light Controversy began.

Transphobia rose to a peak for content creators. Since the algorithm classed her as a trans creator, she received some of the backlash. This affected her channel and her views. Her videos began getting reported and taken down for "adult content," "sexually suggestive content," "inappropriate conduct," etc. These new reports and flags were very interesting considering nothing changed with her posts. She posted a daily vlog about her life being homeless, every day was essentially the same with small steps forward. There was no reason her videos should have been flagged when the prior 200 days were just fine. The anti-trans clan refused to get the message that she was putting something good into the world. But because she was trans, she did not belong.

TikTok became unstable as a business venture with transphobes having the ability to limit her content through fraudulent complaints. She got drawn back into sex work. She still kept her follower base but the content she was allowed to post had to be restricted. One time her video got reported as "dangerous activities" because she was sweeping the area around her tent as cars were driving by.

Another time her video got flagged as dangerous because she hopped a gate to go out into a field to meditate. More strikes increase the risk your account getting banned, so Madam had to limit the type of content she posted. With sex work, she was free to express herself any way she wanted to. Transphobes did not exist because they were not her clientele. After the Dylan Mulvaney Bud Light Controversy, it was her and sex work again.

Groton and Radey (2021) conducted research into the sparsely studied realm of homelessness affecting women. They found that previous studies have shown that the number two mental health conditions affecting women were major depressive disorder and post-traumatic stress disorder. One woman revealed that mental health affected her ability to maintain employment. She stated that she would be at work and randomly burst into tears for unknown reasons.

Homelessness strips you away from the normal world, the normal lens, the normal needs. People living as part of society simply just have things. They keep things for that "what if" or the future "I might need this." While homeless, things can change for you immediately. Your campsite can be ransacked or destroyed. The homeless mind is not thinking to keep items. It thinks about items that it is fine with not holding on to.

Journal Entries from Madam in the Future Starting Her Jobs as a Therapist and Fitness Trainer:

> "I started my first work week as a psychotherapist two weeks ago, and it did not even register to me that I need work clothes. What are "work clothes?" I haven't worn "work clothes" since 2020 while employed at Liberty Mutual before COVID/19 shut the world down and hard launched work from home life. For the last few years, I have been wearing sports bras, leggings, and active shorts.

The last time I wore "work clothes" my gender was male.

I have no idea what type of business casual I even like a woman. Why did it not strike me that I need an entire wardrobe of work clothes? Because I'm still trapped in the homeless mindset. My brain is still disconnected from the average human. I am a therapist, and I have no clothes to dress like one. What do I wear? A dress? What do women call "slacks?" Dress pants? What are the different societal norms for casual, business casual, business, and formal? I have some shopping to do. For the last few years, I only learned how to dress myself in sports activewear.

Day by day I will break free from the homeless mindset. It's not like I can't afford work clothes. If

I needed money to go shopping my TikTok moms would gladly send me money. It just never registered in my mind, "Hey, I am going to need an entire new wardrobe of business and work appropriate casual clothes." That is the homeless mindset. My mind was focused on the major milestones to get me out of homelessness completely ignoring the minuscule pieces that help to build and sustain those major milestones.

I need a purse. For the last few years my gym bag was my purse. My gym bag has held everything I needed. It has gotten me through so much. It enmeshed my personality. But now it's time to upgrade from fitness girl to classy lady. It's time to upgrade from Madam Physique to Madam Ma'am. I need jewelry. I need a lot of things that my mind rendered completely useless because to survive homelessness you must live a life of simplicity. I need regular shoes, not sneakers: casual shoes. For the last few years, I have been wearing active sneakers and heels."

"I got my first job at Equinox Gyms. The hiring manager was a white woman who was very in tune with mental health. During the interview, there was a large three-year gap in my resume. It was quite nerve-racking to tell an employer that I was out of work due to mental health struggles.

My own inner-critic was trying to find a way to make my situation not seem as intense, but there was nothing I could sugarcoat. I told her that I had a very bad psychotic break with PTSD and had to get a new grip on life. She truly appreciated my story and how fitness saved my life. The next day, I accepted a job offer."

"What's the point in holding on to something knowing that it can be taken away? So, you just stop caring. That is the mindset." -Madam

IX. Life

Life was not hard. Life was unlivable. Life was impossible. Life was grueling. What is a life homeless? The entire purpose of life is home. Madam took a look back at the beginning of time. Coming from a Christian background, the beginning of time for her would be the that of Eve and Adam. They had a home at the Garden of Eden. But they too wound up homeless with no clothes.

How did they do it? What did they do? They started over from scratch. They had to figure it out. Madam followed their example. She started over. She found a moderately safe campsite. She bought a tent and made her new home on the sidewalk. Fitness was the only thing keeping her sanity alive. She signed up for a Planet Fitness membership and began her new journey. She was determined to not let homelessness define her. Could she afford Planet Fitness? Barely, but she made enough from sex work that she would be foolish to not spend the money on a gym membership.

A gym membership is an investment. She could shower. She had a private space to put on clothes. She could relax indoors with air conditioning. She had Wi-Fi and electricity to charge her devices. She could find social interactions and build a community. It was the start of a new life.

To start this new life, she had to maintain discipline. She could not afford food at the time and the closest meal service centers was an hour away by bus.

What baffles this author the most was how the government forces a revolving door when it comes to homelessness. How can a person get out of a situation when the system forces them to be surrounded by that very same situation? They market these homeless access centers as "convenience," but that is simply an excuse to group the individuals together and give each a number. "Get in line" is the process that the system uses.

The Women's Center served breakfast around 8:00am, lunch around 11:30am, and afternoon snack around 2:00pm. If Madam wanted to get food, she would have to arrive early because nearly every day they would run out of food. Amazing how a homeless meal service center runs out of food, isn't it?

To accommodate, Madam woke up every day around 7am. She immediately walked to the bus stop to make it in time for breakfast. Most days she would be able to get food and make it back to her tent around 9:30am. After she ate, she would get ready for the gym. Homelessness, PTSD, Depression, Stress: there was a lot going on mentally so Madam spent some time at the gym, a few hours. She usually skipped lunch due to the time conflict, and she never made it for afternoon snack. There was another meal service center that would serve dinner around 4:00pm. That would be her usual dinner spot.

On the days Madam did go back for lunch, around 6 of her daily hours would be spent traveling two and from meal service centers. She would be in line for anywhere from 10-30 minutes. In total, approximately 7 hours of her day could be spent just trying to get daily meals. That is nearly an entire workday for working adults.

On top of the time used for daily meals, Madam was still dealing with severe PTSD symptoms that she needed to heal from. She would meditate for at least 30 minutes to an hour before and after the gym to try and calm her nervous system. She had to do two workouts a day just to manage the traumatic memories replaying in her mind. Her first gym session would be cardio to release the stress pressure from her body. The second session would be strength training to help feel a sense of control over her body. We are looking at approximately 3-4 hours a day working out.

Let's do some arithmetic. Around 7 hours minimum spent on getting three daily meals + 2 hours meditating + 3 hours doing fitness for mental health = at least 12 hours/day just simply trying to cope with homelessness. On top of that, this system expects a mentally ill homeless person to go to work.

She tried. She had interviews. She could not lie to get employment. She had a viral public docu-series. Unfortunately, capitalism does not accept people who need help. Capitalism needs slavery. Madam was not a suitable candidate for slavery because she gave "unstable." But she needed help to make her stable.

Question for capitalism, how can one get stable without employment? Her resume was impeccable. Her work experience was irrefutable. They mentally refused to accommodate the state of her life. Aren't companies supposed to abide by the Americans with Disabilities Act? What made her an unqualified candidate? She was disabled and that disability destroyed the life she once knew.

There had to be another meaning to life. She was determined to find that other meaning. She never found that other meaning. She found a fulfillment of living. Living should not feel like a starving homeless stomach. It should feel full. It should feel lively. Every day, Madam was determined to feel full. In order to feel full, she had to examine what makes her feel empty: being disabled.

How do you live with a disability? In 2025, Soraya, Norouzi Seyed Hossini, and Saffari completed a study into the journey of personality traits and life satisfaction with disabled athletes. In fact, your personality traits have significant influence towards your attitude and perceptions of your environment

(Soraya, et. al, 2025). The research has also found that while not minimizing the damaging effect becoming disabled has on an individual's life satisfaction, the extent of the effect can be predetermined or moderated based on an individual's personality traits prior to the disability.

There is one thing that prevented Madam from feeling full in life: she disagreed with having a disability. That mere thought of being disabled at 24 years old seemed very vacuous for a person with a college education. Disagreeing with having a disability does nothing to mend the effects of such disability and prohibits the insight to improve life conditions. Soraya, Norouzi Seyed Hossini, and Saffari (2025) indicate individuals that are able to moderately agree with their disability exhibit higher levels of life satisfaction compared to individuals who do not moderately agree with their disability. Moderately is a crucial word in the above finding.

Living with a disability does not mean one has to immediately capitulate to the drastic life change. It is an adjustment, but simply accepting the presence of such change could be enough to moderately agree with the existence of a disability. For Madam, accepting this disability meant comprehending that her life would no longer be the same.

One thing about Madam: she's a fighter. Growing up she was the rebel child, the black sheep of the family. In school, she was forced to assert her dominance. In life, she had to be rewarded respect. Having a disability was just another challenge. What were the worst side effects of her PTSD? Flashbacks.

Elevated Nervous System. Hypervigilance. Intrusive Memories. Anger/Irritability. Nothing Madam could not handle.

Triaging these side effects based on ability to cure helped Madam to adjust to living with a disability. Finding work was not a viable solution at this time. That would only allow her to continue escaping via distraction with having a disability. *What do you mean I am no longer able to work?* Well, yes. It is called dis-abled to work, not able to work. Dis-ability to work, no ability to work.

Self-soothing activities should help her nervous system relax and calm down. The first thing needed was to slow down the uncontrollable shaking. Grounding techniques and activities became a required daily task. The yoga pose Shavasana was an essential portion of her morning routine.

Intrusive memories was another manageable side effect. Intrusive memories usually arise from triggers whether aware or silent. Most silent triggers include peripheral vision and smell. Redirection of the brain became a skilled practice. After redirection, grounding techniques followed such as painting, sketching, writing, etc.

The anger and irritability side effects of PTSD were actually emotional side effects of flashbacks, hypervigilance, elevated nervous system, etc. Leftover are the flashbacks and hypervigilance. Routine mental health treatment to include psychotropic medications helped with the hypervigilance. Madam's brain has seen things that the average human brain will never compute to reality. This exposure to alternate realities heightens her brain's defense systems. As of the time of this book, the remedy for hypervigilance and flashbacks are currently still in works.

"What's the point in holding on to something knowing that it can be taken away? So, you just stop caring. That is the mindset." -Madam

X. Finding Your Salvation

"Un-loved. Un-nurtured. Un-worthy. Forgotten. Pitiful.: these are the feelings that can make or break your salvation while homeless. Every religion or spiritual belief I have ever read about always tells the person to see the positive. A famous saying that I have heard repeatedly in my life is along the lines of: If you think you can or you can't, you're right." -Madam

If you think you cannot make it out of homelessness, your brain will never highlight the opportunities to help you get out of it: so, you're right. If you think you can make it out of homelessness, your brain will illuminate every opportunity to help you get out of it: so, you're right. If you think you are un-loved, your brain will register every environmental factor to make you believe you're right. If you think you are loved, your brain will illuminate every factor to show you you're right.

Most people confuse faith with "tests." That comes from a classist western society that has morphed our brains into believing that you are only worthy if you "pass" something. Faith is an experience. Homelessness does not "test" your faith. If that is the case, then why haven't the people who have never experienced homelessness been "tested?" Homelessness allows one to experience faith at an abnormal level that the general society will never have the opportunity to experience.

Salvation was not something Madam believed was possible for her. Attending Christian school, it was engrained in her mind that being a member of the LGBT+ community was ungodly. The teachings she received at Christian school did not align with her own personal views. As a child, Madam never cared if somebody was LGBT. Children are innately selfish and selfless at the same time. Unless it bothers a child specifically, they do not care.

Once Madam's parents agreed on public school enrollment, her entire salvation changed. Madam immediately became agnostic. Looking back, this was more of an angry rebellion against Christianity. She despised everything that she was taught in Christian school. She felt free to develop her own independent spiritual beliefs. This independence followed her through homelessness. She used homelessness as a way to prove whether or not a God existed. What she found was even more spiritual than she could ever imagine.

After her suicide attempt, Madam got rid of everything that she traveled with. No phone. No identity. No clothes. She cried, all day and night. This was a level of heartbreak she had never experienced before. Her heart ached, and ached, and ached. After crying a thunderstorm for a few days, the sun finally rose. She looked up with tears rolling down her face. She stared at the sun and asked, *"What now?"*

While sitting in sorrow on her favorite boulder, a friend came to visit her: a pigeon. This pigeon had a metallic coat. It just stood there, looking at her. Suddenly, a feeling of calmness encroached her. *"I will be okay,"* she felt. She spent the day staring into the horizon. There was nothing on her mind, just complete peace and tranquility.

Another occasion: It was the end of the month, and she ran out of food stamps. She was alone on the sidewalk. What to do? One option was to put on that freakum dress and go work that corner really quick. She could also go out and meet a guy to go home with. She could post a sex ad. There were options to make a quick buck. She decided to go out and work the night shift.

With it still being daytime, it was time to go to the gym. As soon as she was getting ready to leave for the gym, this elderly Asian lady stopped by her tent with a cart. In the cart were bags filled with bagels, bananas, and water bottles. The Asian lady spoke very minimal English. She yelled, *"Bagel?"* and pointed to the cart. Madam was starving. How did she find her? Did she live in the neighborhood? This lady said she was from a church and described the location not too far away. The church was at least a 20-minute walk.

This elderly lady was just out walking miles just giving out bagels to the homeless and her spirit gravitated her to deviate from her normal route until she reached Madam. Madam asked for multiple bagels, bananas, and water. She let Madam take as many items as she wanted. Now, Madam had breakfast and a post workout meal. The excitement consumed her. She had two options now, stay and rationalize the food she had, or go out and try to make money for more food. Madam decided to stay and rationalize the food she had.

Another occasion: The same day as the Asian elder with the bagel Madam returned from the gym and took a nap. About two hours later she was sitting outside enjoying the time pass. A man was walking by. When he saw Madam, he immediately drew himself in. *"I have something I want to ask you,"* he said.

"What is it?" Madam responded.

"How much would it be if I could fool around with you?"

"Like sex?"

"Yeah."

"I start at $100, what are you trying to do?"

"I only have $50. I don't know how to say this, but I've never, you know, gave head before and I've wanted to try it, but these girls out here got stuff on their lips and look a mess. You look like you don't have anything. I feel safer with you."

"You want to give me fellatio?" Madam asked.

"Yeah, if that's cool with you?"

"How much you got again?" Madam inquired.

"I only got $50 but after my social security deposits I can come back and bring you some more."

Madam needed the money. She agreed. The man gave her the money, and she taught him how to correctly give fellatio.

Right after, Madam went straight to the grocery store and got some food. She got peanut butter and jelly, lunchables, and lunch meat. This food should last a few days. She even had leftover cash in case she needed to make another grocery run later in the week. The next day, the same Asian elder came back to her tent. She gave Madam more bagels, bananas, and water. By the end of this delivery, Madam was satisfied.

She had enough food to rationalize until she received more food stamps.

Madam started to feel like she was being saved by a higher power. Somebody or something was definitely watching over her. Whatever was watching over her was tired of seeing her struggling out on the street.

Another day the same Asian elder returned with more water, bagels, and bananas. By this time Madam considered herself officially. She asked Madam, *"What are you? Boy or girl?"* Madam responded, *"Girl."*

The Asian elder asked, *"Oh okay, what is your name?"*

"Madam."

"Madam?" The Asian elder asked.

"Madam."

"Yes yes, Madam, beautiful. Beautiful name. You are beautiful."

The two talked for a few more minutes. After this conversation officially referred to this Asian elder as her "Asian mom."

Her Asian mom came to visit her daily. Every morning, she would stop by with her cart filled with bagels, bananas, & water. *"Madam! Madam!"* She would call out. Asian mom did not know just how much of a lifesaver she actually was. Most days, Madam would wake up hungry, sometimes starving. She would wait patiently, hoping that her Asian mom would arrive with food.

On the days Madam needed food most, *"Rose! Rose!"* she would hear outside her tent. Madam jumped up ecstatic for her daily breakfast delivery. On one special occasion, her Asian mom brought a friend: an Asian man. The was more fluent in English than her Asian mom so he and Madam had a more thorough conversation. He introduced himself and explained he was from the same church as her Asian mom. He said her newly found mom has shared so much about the homeless people she meets on her daily walks and inspired more members of the church to help with deliveries.

Another occasion: Madam experienced a harrowing PTSD episode. She became filled with rage. It consumed her entire being. Her Obamaphone ended up freezing doing a task for her TikTok moms. Now, the normal person with a balanced mindset would simply try to restart the phone. For somebody experiencing a PTSD-aggression manic episode, their mind is not balanced. Symbiosis is not intact. The sympathetic nervous system is activated. This overwhelming aggression must be expelled from their body.

Madam slammed the phone on the concrete ground again, and again, and again. The more she slammed it, the more excited she became. To explain, the excitement does not come from the actual damage being done. This excitement comes from immense rage finally being released. PTSD-aggression episodes can be compared to a pressure cooker. Finally, the intense emotion is being released, and their brain is returning to symbiosis. Thus, leading to the feeling of joy because they are slowly regaining control of their body.

As with every human being after experiencing an episode of anger, it is now time to reflect, process, and seek remedy.

"Ughh...why did I do that? Now I have no phone. How am I going to stay in contact with my moms? They know if I don't post then something is wrong. Ughhh...I'm so stupid. Ughhh...I can't help it. I just get so mad." - Madam

These thoughts raced through her mind. The next day, Madam went to an Obamaphone table and got a new phone. She went back to her tent and showed her moms what she did. One mom did not live too far from her tent. She showed up to Madam's tent.

"Hello? Is anyone home?" The mom asked. *"I'm from TikTok. I brought you some stuff."*

Madam opened up her tent and came outside.

"Hi, I'm Catarina. I have been following you, and I saw that you broke your phone, so I brought you an old one and some other stuff."

Madam's face lit up. It was an iPhone. Catarina's daughter just recently upgraded and had that phone at the house.

"Now you don't have to record on that terrible camera," Catarina said with a chuckle. *"Me and my daughter watch you every night before bed. You have given us a way to bond. I wanted to tell you how much we love you and how much inspiration you give us."*

This was the beginning of a loving relationship with a new mother figure. Catarina and Madam went to the gym together a few times a month, and afterwards, they would get a large protein meal from a nearby restaurant. It was just the salvation that Madam needed to tell her to keep going because someone was watching over her.

This launched the official start of her TikTok channel. Moms, aunts, and sisters began closing rings to uplift their newfound family member. One by one they ushered in a new era of love, light, and positivity. She finally had friends. She began to feel the love of "it takes a village."

Richardson et al. (2026) conducted research into suicidal ideations and thoughts within the African American community. They emphasized the meaning of radical hope, which they defined as "a firm conviction in the capacity of communities of color to collectively heal and transform with a steadfast belief in a better future despite oppressive forces and psychological harm." The article goes on to discuss that hope provides an expectation that one's needs will be met such as long as one perseveres. Hope can bend reality, influence outcomes, and shatter illusions.

Hope can be your greatest savior. It provides you with an actionable vision. It shows you a new way to view things. With this comes your new beginning. No matter your beliefs, there always comes a time in your life when you feel saved. Find Your Salvation.

"What's the point in holding on to something knowing that it can be taken away? So, you just stop caring. That is the mindset." -Madam

XI. Living Your Truth

The easiest path to begin anew is to let people know where you are in life. Humans are humans. We all have a natural inclination to be there for one another, even some random you just met crying at the grocery store. We all have our tough times, and we all like to feel that feeling when we do something good. There is no better feeling than feeling like you have helped somebody out.

So let them in. Let people see the real you. Do not hide. Do not shy away. Let them see the broken parts because that person you are talking to just might be the one able to repair you right there. Vulnerability is the bonding agent for trust.

When Madam chose the location for her tent, it was not at random. She needed the help of humans. She needed the neighborhood to know that she was struggling, she was hurting, she was in a crisis, and she needed their help.

At first, the neighborhood was uneasy, but she knew she had to let them into her life so they could lower their guard and see the human within homelessness. The first thing Madam knew to do was keep the area clean. Cleanliness provides the aura of welcoming. Before guests arrive, our natural human instincts tell us to clean up prior to their arrival. Madam went to the dollar store and got a broom. Just a small $1.25 + tax out of the $220/mo. she received from disability aid. Every morning, she swept the sidewalk and picked up anything that needed to be thrown away.

It was not long before word got around the neighborhood that a young girl was experiencing homelessness under the bridge just around the corner. The first thought she wanted associated with her was, “she keeps the area clean.”

Next, Madam needed to breathe life into her home. Despite contrary thought processes, homeless people do have a home. It may be a small box. It may be a tent. It may even be an open sidewalk. It is a home. Madam went walking around the neighborhood to find furniture that was thrown out. To residents, that furniture was broken and useless, but to somebody experiencing homelessness that furniture is a brand-new table, a brand-new chair, a brand-new decoration.

After she arranged her furniture, she sat outside. She let the neighborhood get a good look at her. She let them get used to her. She let them be the natural curious humans that we all are.

It was not long before they would stop by and talk to her. Some would be driving home and stop traffic just to introduce themselves. Her favorite would be when somebody was returning from grocery shopping and said, "I got this for you." It meant that she was on somebody's mind. To somebody, she was worthy of being cared for.

It was not long before word spread throughout the neighborhood about Madam and her life, and the natural helping human instincts came flooding in. They saw her in her gym clothes. They noticed how she chose to camp at a specific location with access to the gym and grocery stores. They pieced together that she was trying to better her life and needed a village to help raise this inner child.

The neighborhood invited her over for breakfast, lunch, dinners, parties, holidays. It was the most promising sign of humanity one could ever witness. All because she let them see her truth: she was hurting, she was struggling, most importantly, she was trying.

"[People] from high-risk backgrounds, who formed bonds with caring and trusting other adults, turned out to be more resilient, than those who did not form such connections" (Reupert, et. al, 2022). You have to let people in. You must remember that the same way you have a curious mind, so does every other human. We all crave to know other people's life experience, what they have been through.

Due to insurmountable trauma, Madam was not good at verbalizing what she was going through, but she always made sure to show it in one way or another. The people she knows to befriend are the ones that get these trauma subtleties because that shows that they deeply understand and connect with somebody like her.

On the outside Madam might look fine, but is she? Where is she getting money from? Deductive reasoning can tell you that she is involved in sex work. Why would somebody like her be in sex work? Inductive reasoning can tell you that obviously there is some internal struggle she is dealing with that cannot be observed by the naked eye.

Why is a girl like her on the streets and not in a shelter? Either she cannot get in one, or she has some mental issues going on. A lot of moms would recognize that and find a way to safely weave that into the conversation.

Madam tried many times to get out of sex work. She struggled to get a call back in the only industry that she knew how to manage her PTSD symptoms. Living in your truth does not mean that you need to wear a scarlet letter on your chest. Knowing about other people's lives interests us. It is all a part of this shared human experience.

We cannot share this human experience if you do not share yourself. Of course there are boundaries. Family was always off limits for her. Family is an extremely complicated topic for a lot of people. Madam would only speak openly about her birth father because the two of them will never have a relationship with him again.

As humans, we all understand certain things are private such as family. You have to give humanity the same curiosity you give yourself. Have you ever worked a job with somebody not in your age group whether older or younger? What life role did you automatically step in for that person? Mom? Niece? Grandpa? Cousin?

If you are going through a breakup, speak to your work mom about that, especially if she is divorced. If you are having kid problems, speak to your work niece about that, especially if they are of the same generation. “In many societies, nonparental caretaking is either the norm or occurs frequently” (Reupert, et. al, 2022).

The best personal conversations you can have are the ones where those conversations are constricted to time and place with people not in our regular circle. Sometimes we just need an empty vessel to drop off all this trauma into and then return back to our routine life.

Living your truth does not mean pretending like you are not bothered. It means showing us how you are empowering yourself from that situation. Madam is a fitness trainer. She sees plenty of women come into the gym, but the ones she pays attention to the most are older women. They are in there releasing anger that they never even knew they could feel. They see Madam as a symbol of strength.

A lot are single moms. Some were lost in their life. But they made their way into the gym and now they are found because they finally found themselves again. They ask Madam for advice. Some even ask her about her gender transition. They turn into that natural curious human being that we all are. Madam always answers all of their questions because sharing your experience promotes the shared human experience.

In Living Your Truth, you feel seen. You feel heard. You feel human. One day Madam was in the gym. She just finished an amazing workout at her home gym. Every regular club member knew her. Every staff member knew her. Since Madam was homeless, she used the resources that came with her gym membership. This included the shower.

Madam exited the shower after cleansing herself and walked into the changing stall. A few seconds later she hears a distant voice, "*I cannot shower with you in here. This is the women's locker room, and you need to go to the men's locker room."* Bewildered, Madam believed the lady to be speaking to another person who may have walked into the locker room. A few seconds later the voice gets louder and closer. *"Are they talking to me?"* Madam asks herself.

A few seconds later, this lady bangs on the stall door startling Madam. She repeats the same message. Madam looks at the door to see a shadow begin to encroach the floor. The lady gets on all fours and looks underneath the stall, yelling the same message.

"Are you crazy?" Madam yells in shock and fear.

The lady says the same message as she gets up off the floor and bangs on the stall door again, this time trying to shake the door open. Madam jumps up in shock. She rushes to put on her leggings and opens the stall door.

"If you have an issue with me being in here you go tell management. You do not come peeping under stalls trying to get a closer look at me. That is harassment and stalking." Madam explains.

The deranged lady has her mind on repeat. She keeps repeating the same message, *"You're a man and you don't need to be in this restroom."* Madam, being more mature, decided to walk to go get management involved.

As Madam turns, this deranged lady pushes Madam to "hurry up." Appalled, Madam turns at her and firmly says, *"Don't touch me. I have PTSD and you touching me triggers me. Don't ever touch me."*

They take a few more steps and this lady pushes Madam again yelling the same thing. In an automatic reaction Madam pushes the deranged lady off of her. The lady loses her balance and strikes her head against the wall. Here come the tears. She begins wailing and screaming, *"You hit me! You hit me!"*

"I did not hit you. I pushed you off of me after I repeatedly told you not to touch me," Madam says.

At the same time management and stuff run into the locker room due to the screams. *"What's going on?"* The manager asks.

"She has a problem with me being in here, and instead of going to you she wanted to be captain and remove me herself," Madam responds.

"Why is she screaming?" the manager asks.

"I don't know. She kept pushing me out. I told her to quit touching me. After repeated pushes I reacted like anybody would and pushed her off of me. Her head hit the wall and now she's trying to play victim," Madam explains.

This deranged lady told management to call the police so she could file a report. She also requested paramedics to check out the cut on her head from striking the wall. Madam finished getting ready, and the police still have not arrived. Management told her that she could leave if she wanted. Madam refused. If the police only hear one side of the story, then the complainant is automatically right. Police took over an hour to respond, but finally they came. Four officers came to investigate the situation.

Madam told them exactly what you have just read. She got out the shower, the deranged lady started banging on the stall door and even violated her right to privacy by getting on all fours and looking under the stall. Then the lady started pushing Madam which caused a reactionary push back. The police asked how the lady received a cut on her head. After further investigation, it looked like the lady received instant karma. Her head hit the corner of one of the posted signs on the wall which caused the laceration.

After a few minutes of waiting, the lead investigating officer came over and told Madam that the deranged lady requested Madam be put under arrest for battery. Madam was appalled. The officer did say that both of their stories matched, except the deranged lady refused to admit that she was pushing Madam.

Looking at the facts of the case, the deranged lady was the instigator. She had every chance to go get management instead of taking matters into her own hands, she violated Madam's right to privacy, and Madam was the one who opted to go get management. The officers on scene believed Madam's side of the story. After consulting with the sergeant on scene, the police decided that either both Madam and the deranged lady would be going to jail or nobody goes to jail. Once the police told the deranged lady of their decision, she opted that nobody goes to jail.

The case was closed and filed as a declination to prosecute and documentation only. Living in your truth, your presence will automatically trigger those not living in their truth. Over time, you will naturally run into other people like you and then you both will help each other achieve an even greater sense of awareness.

Madam's gym family was filled with remorse that Madam had to go through that situation. After this incident, Madam took about a week off from the gym. When she came back, she was welcomed with open arms. You deserve to feel seen. Humans seek connection, community, belonging, love.

The connections you bond let you know that you are not alone and this is a very natural human experience. The new community gives you a new home base: a new part of the world to live in and belong. Love is the ingredient that ties everything together, always. This new state of being begins to take over. You love it. It feels like you. So now you start to truly live in it. Now, you are living in and supported in your truth.

"What's the point in holding on to something knowing that it can be taken away? So, you just stop caring. That is the mindset." -Madam

XII. Becoming the New You

She doesn't even know what belongs in a bedroom. What color scheme does she go for? What theme do she want? What items does she get? Madam had to Google "what essentials do you need for a bedroom?" It has been so long since she actually lived in one. Her life was reduced to minimalism. Bedroom accessories were unnecessary. She only remembered that she needed pillows because a friend asked her if she needed some. That is how long she has slept without pillows. Her brain forgot they were an essential part of sleep.

When you are starting over from literally nothing, every single dollar counts. The twenty dollars that she could have used to buy pillows would have gotten her enough food from the dollar store to last one week.

The makeshift pillows out of piled clothes were just fine.

Becoming the New You is just that: A New You. A You that you no longer recognize…because it is New. A lot of people try to get their old life back, but why would you want your old life back? That old life is what led you to homelessness, led you to trauma, led you to pain. Yes, we can blame systemic issues, but the way your old life was intertwined throughout those systemic issues still led you to homelessness, trauma, pain.

Why not try something new? A new impenetrable you that the past will never be an option. Life revolves around new: new behaviors, new scenery, new thought patterns, new friends, new additions to your family, new jobs, new careers, new ideas, new furniture, a new residence, new, new, new. It is only in the new that life can continue to flourish.

Think of life as a tree. A tree loses its leaves every autumn season. A tree loses unnecessary ill–fitting leaves constantly throughout the year. Sometimes those leaves are forcibly plucked or removed by an outside force: animals, humans, wind, rain, hail, etc. In life, our leaves are forcibly plucked by an outside force such as the forces of nature or a major traumatic event.

We lose unnecessary ill-fitting leaves constantly throughout the year through items breaking, breakups, much needed upgrading, etc. If you believe in New Year's Resolutions, Birthday New Habits, Spring Cleaning, etc., then you have a mandatory annual unnecessary ill-fitting leaf shedding season. New, new, new.

This author will use themself as an example since our brain retains the best information from relatable human experiences. I do not believe in New Year's Resolutions because I install habits throughout the year. I do, however, do a mandatory birthday shedding to set my intentions for the new year of age I am stepping into. When an item breaks, I simply throw it away and get something better. If I need to replace it with a replica, then I get a different color.

New, new, new. When the forces of nature force its weight on me, I do not fight it, no matter the financial risk, no matter the stress and strain it will cause, I always listen. This keeps my life, my mind, and my heart fresh. It keeps me in an opportunistic mindset- always looking for more, for better. If you want further insight and guidance, then do not be scared to book me for a life coaching session.

Back to Homeless Fortune, the easiest way to become this new you is to see yourself in the best light. Now, confirm your reality. We have all done things we are ashamed of. We have all made poor decisions. We have all had a bitter era of misery. It starts with internal honesty.

How can you become this new version of you if you cannot see your own reflection and the muck accumulated on it in the mirror? Still look at yourself in the best light. That shows you everything you are capable of. All of the lit pathways that are still available to you. It is beautiful, isn't it? Now walk in that best light. Actively choose that best light. It starts with you. All you have to do is start.

Once you have chosen that path, I want you to look again. Look around, see the trees, see the road, see the beauty. Who do you see? Sometimes we want to invite people on the path who were not in the original picture simply because we want them to enjoy the beauty. But what we cannot see is that person is carrying their own dark cloud. Their dark cloud can slowly taint and infect your beautiful lit path.

Have you seen Spider-Man? Do you remember how he became Venom? That dark substance got stuck, and if he did not remove it within a certain timeframe then the darkness would consume him. Apply this same philosophy to your new start. Because it is a breath of fresh air, I know you do not want any more pollution.

Becoming the new you is taking everything you have gone through and also noting the faults of yours that played a role. Have you ever taken a Victimology class? If not, have you ever been in a car accident and had to deal with the other person's insurance? Did they tell you they were only accepting 80% fault, and you are responsible for the other 20% of damages? Victimology teaches us the same.

If you leave your bike on your porch without a lock and it is stolen overnight, then Victimology tells you that you subjected yourself to being victimized. This in no way, shape, form, or direction is implying that your bike getting stolen is your fault. It highlights a level of awareness that we as humans must develop to survive in a world filled with sin. So, look at the negative things that happened in your old life. Where did your old self intentionally or subconsciously contribute to any of the mishaps and wrongdoings?

Did you have another drink when you knew you should have stopped? Did you go back to that toxic partner after you left the first time? Did you spend recklessly when you knew you needed to save? Victimology does not in any way take blame off the real at-fault person, system, or object. But it does provide a framework to help you protect yourself from any future reoccurrences.

We learn the best by looking into someone else's life. So, this author will tell you some of my mishaps. I should not have clinical-PTSD. When I was in my undergraduate program, I landed a position in the office of a United States Congressional Representative. She decided not to seek re-election and thus began the job relocation efforts around the office. The District Manager knew somebody who she felt I would be perfect for.

The job was mine. All I had to do was turn in the paperwork. The fear of jumping out the nest from my family caused me to turn down the opportunity. That led me right back into the arms of my abuser and his manipulation tactics. It all went downhill from there until I finally set myself free 4 years later after our big blowout.

I had to accept that I missed a job opportunity that would have secured my future all to chase a love from my father that I would never ever receive. As of writing this paragraph, I have set forth the motions to rectify that decision and get me on a path that I am proud of.

It is not easy. I am in the process of "catching up." But one day I will be caught up, and you could be too.

Becoming the new you is not a moment. It is a lifestyle choice. You have to actively, continuously choose this new you. You have to purposefully walk in this new path you chose. Of course it is not easy, you are not a child anymore. Children are like sponges. They are malleable and soak up anything: good or bad. Their brain is developed enough to understand the bad things they soak up will actually deteriorate them. They cannot tell that the good things they soak up are actually cleansing and purifying them.

You are an adult now. You live your life in a means of familiarity and comfortability: no matter if that is good or bad for you.

Breaking the habit of comfortability is hard. But you know what else is hard? Living a life in the state of misery for another two, five, or ten years. Choose your hard. You know what was hard for some people? College entrance exams such as the SAT and ACT. You know what is hard for others? Simply walking away from a life that no longer suits them. Since you are already reading, do you mind if I read you really quick?

You are only living this life of comfortability (knowing it is bad, toxic, or unhealthy) due to your own protective mechanisms. What are you so afraid of? Who hurt you so deep that caused you to bear a time of pain that you do not even realize you transformed your own life into a life of pain? Because now you are hurting you. You are hurting your future. You are hurting your happiness.

We usually only hear the phrase "people change" in a negative light. We usually only hear the phrase "why you acting brand new" in a negative light. What could such a negative assumption come from? People break bones, people become paralyzed, people develop cancer, yet we do not attach a negative change fixture to them. Now think a broken heart, numb feelings, sickness due to stress and trauma.

What causes society to assume someone who simply wants better for their independent life is negative? Because you no longer suit the role they need you for. Read that sentence again. In their eyes, it is a negative thing because that attachment string has been severed. The new you is for your life experience and yours only.

"What's the point in holding on to something knowing that it can be taken away? So, you just stop caring. That is the mindset." -Madam

"Build something that nobody can take away from you. So you can actually care. That is our new mindset." -Pharose King, this author

I told you ***our*** new mindset. Now it's time for you to come up with your own personal mindset. Once you think of something, write it down below:

Chapter-Themed Scholarly References

(Chapters are written from author's own framework and not from references. All references were inserted after as complementary.)

Chapter 1:

Seager, M. (2011). Homelessness is more than houselessness: A psychologically-minded approach to inclusion and rough sleeping. Mental Health and Social Inclusion, 15(4), 183–189. https://doi.org/10.1108/20428301111186822

Chapter 2:

Maizes, V., & Weil, A. (Hosts). (2024, November 13). Neurogenic tremors for trauma release with David Berceli, PhD (No. 55) [Audio podcast episode]. In Body of Wonder. Andrew Weil Center for Integrative Medicine.

https://awcim.arizona.edu/podcast/episode55_berceli.html

Chapter 3:

Palmer, P. J. (2004). Finding your soul. *Spirituality & Health*, 38-43.

Chapter 4:

Fisher, M. R., Turner, C., McFarland, W., Breslow, A. S., Wilson, E. C., & Arayasirikul, S. (2023). Through a Different Lens: Occupational Health of Sex-Working Young Trans Women. *Transgender health*, *8*(2), 200–206. https://doi.org/10.1089/trgh.2021.0109

Chapter 5:

Sanders, T. (2001). Female street workers, sexual violence, and protection strategies. *Journal of Sexual Aggression*, 7(1), 5–18. https://doi.org/10.1080/13552600108413318

Chapter 6:

Hamermesh, D. S., & Soss, N. M. (1974). An economic theory of suicide. Journal of Political Economy, 82(1), 83–98. https://doi.org/10.1086/260171

Chapter 7:

Washington, O. G. M., Moxley, D. P., Garriott, L., & Weinberger, J. P. (2009). Five dimensions of faith and spiritually of older African American women transitioning out of homelessness.

Journal of Religion and Health, *48*(4), 431–444. https://doi.org/10.1007/s10943-008-9198-6

Chapter 8:

Groton, D., & Radey, M. (2021). "I've Been through It": Assessing Employment Barriers among Unaccompanied Women Experiencing Homelessness. *Social Work Research*, *45*(2), 88–100. https://doi.org/10.1093/swr/svab003

Chapter 9:

Soraya, F., Norouzi Seyed Hossini, R., & Saffari, M. (2025). Redefining possibilities: a journey into personality traits, serious leisure, and life satisfaction among athletes with physical disabilities. *Managing Sport & Leisure*, *30*(5), 998–

1014.

https://doi.org/10.1080/23750472.2024.2345371

Chapter 10:

Richardson, S. C., Gryglewicz, K., Williams, J. A., Phipps-Bennett, M., Dennis, S., Browne, N., Trujillo, A., Carlisle, C., Nail, M., & Karver, M. (2026). The Pursuit of Radical Hope: Suicidal Help-Seeking Behaviors Among Black Adolescents and Caregivers. *Journal of Clinical Child and Adolescent Psychology : The Official Journal for the Society of Clinical Child and Adolescent Psychology, American Psychological Association, Division 53*, *55*(2), 345–359. https://doi.org/10.1080/15374416.2025.2579278

Chapter 11:

Reupert, A., Straussner, S. L., Weimand, B., & Maybery, D. (2022). It Takes a Village to Raise a Child: Understanding and Expanding the Concept of the "Village". Frontiers in public health, 10, 756066. https://doi.org/10.3389/fpubh.2022.756066

Chapter 12:

Sjöblom, M., Öhrling, K., Prellwitz, M., & Kostenius, C. (2016). Health throughout the lifespan: The phenomenon of the inner child reflected in events during childhood experienced by older persons. *International journal of qualitative studies on health and well-*

being, *11*, 31486.

https://doi.org/10.3402/qhw.v11.31486

How to Catch Up on My Crazy Life

Visual Blog Website: MadamPhysique.com

Social Media (at the time of this book):

- **TikTok:** @TheMadamPhysique
- **Instagram:** @TheMadamPhysique
- **YouTube:** @MadamPhysique

MadamPhysique.com is the hub to connect you to all things related to and of me, straight from the source.

www.ingramcontent.com/pod-product-compliance
Lightning Source LLC
LaVergne TN
LVHW100140061126
851857LV00010B/168